C000153140

Making an Impact in HIV and AIDS

Making an Impact in HIV and AIDS
NGO Experiences of Scaling up

Jocelyn DeJong

ITDG
PUBLISHING

Published by ITDG Publishing
103–105 Southampton Row, London WC1B 4HL, UK
www.itdgpublishing.org.uk

© The Population Council Inc. 2003

First published in 2003

ISBN 1 85339 539 0

All rights reserved. No part of this publication may be reprinted or
reproduced or utilized in any form or by any electronic, mechanical,
or other means, now known or hereafter invented, including
photocopying and recording, or in any information storage or
retrieval system, without the written permission of the publishers.

A catalogue record for this book is available from the British Library.

ITDG Publishing is the publishing arm of the Intermediate
Technology Development Group.
Our mission is to build the skills and capacity of people in
developing countries through the dissemination of information in
all forms, enabling them to improve the quality of their lives and
that of future generations.

Typeset by J&L Composition, Filey, North Yorkshire
Printed in Great Britain by Bell & Bain, Glasgow

Contents

Acknowledgements

The work culminating in this publication was very much a team effort and thanks are due to all those who participated in the process along the way. The idea behind it originated with Chris Castle of Horizons (which, along with the International HIV/AIDS Alliance, commissioned this research). Without his dedication to the project, his enthusiastic support and insightful comments throughout his tireless reading of multiple drafts, this book would not have come to light. Chris and colleagues at both Horizons and the International HIV/AIDS Alliance undertook the planning for the Horizons/Alliance seminar held in September 2000 in Windsor, UK, at which case studies of NGOs' scaling-up experiences documented here were presented. They used their enormous knowledge of the HIV/AIDS field to select appropriate organizations to invite to that seminar which would exemplify the challenges of scaling up in all aspects of that field.

Each participant organization at that seminar (listed in the Appendix) invested substantial time in documenting its scaling-up experiences in advance of the event. Discussions at the seminar about the challenges and objectives of scaling up greatly informed the arguments in this book, and I am grateful to each participant for his or her frank and insightful comments. At the suggestion of the publisher, references to comments made by the seminar participants have been omitted from the main text of the book, but unless otherwise cited, all direct quotes by individuals are from that seminar.

I am particularly indebted to the International HIV/AIDS Alliance team in the UK working on this project. Special and profound thanks are due to Sue Lucas, who, when this work was initiated, was working at the International HIV/AIDS Alliance. Sue joined Chris in providing intellectual and moral support to the efforts of producing this publication and, while at the Alliance, arranged for its publication by the ITDG. Throughout the process she provided key insights based on her extensive experience of working with NGOs in HIV/AIDS, and subsequently contributed substantial time filling gaps, adding new ideas and providing constructive criticisms. Helen Parry provided ideas and support to the drafting, and generously offered her time in reviewing successive drafts. Jeff O'Malley was instrumental in the development of this project and throughout the process, provided useful insights. In particular, we are grateful to him for the extensive case study on the International HIV/AIDS Alliance. The discussion in Chapter 10 on trends in donor priorities in HIV/AIDS draws on that case study, as does the discussion of the evolution in 'best practice' in HIV/AIDS in the same chapter. Vic Salas, also at the International HIV/AIDS Alliance, shared useful first-hand information on the Cambodian situation, reflected particularly in Chapter 5. Kieran Daly provided useful references and leads on the role of NGO–private sector partnerships discussed in Chapter 5.

Given the lack of economic analysis of scaling up as applied to NGOs active in HIV/AIDS, Horizons and the International HIV/AIDS Alliance commissioned a health economist, Lilani Kumaranayake at the London School of Hygiene and Tropical Medicine, to review the text and insert information on how to approach costing analyses in HIV/AIDS. I am grateful to Lilani for providing the material for the section on economists' perspectives in Chapter 7, and for her other comments on the text. Thanks are also due to Stefano Bertozzi of the Instituto Nacional de Salud Publica (Mexico), who provided useful insights on the particularities of costing NGO programmes in HIV/AIDS on the basis of his ongoing work in this area.

Particular thanks are due to two seminar participants, Paurvi Bhatt (formerly of USAID and currently with the Abbot Laboratories Fund Step Forward Program) and Margarita Quevedo (of Corporación Kimirina in Ecuador) for reviewing earlier drafts of this publication. Margarita also provided constructive comments on successive drafts.

At my own institution, the Institute for Development Policy and Management at the University of Manchester, David Hulme encouraged me to get involved in this project, based on his earlier work on scaling up NGO efforts in development more broadly. Thanks are due to him for this, as well as comments made on the early ideas behind it.

A number of people were particularly helpful in producing this publication. Garry Robson at the International HIV/AIDS Alliance designed and assembled earlier drafts of this publication meticulously. In Manchester, I am particularly grateful to Elaine Mercer for her careful and patient editing of successive drafts. At Horizons, both Eva Roca and Malea Hoepf provided administrative support.

Thanks are also due to Helen Marsden at ITDG Publishing, who gave useful comments on successive drafts and shepherded this project through to fruition.

This study was made possible through support provided by the US Agency for International Development. Its publication was made possible through the support of the UK Department for International Development (DFID) and Merck & Co Inc.

Last but certainly not least, this book would not have come to light without the personal and intellectual support of Tariq Tell.

The author and publishers are grateful to Blackwell Publishers Ltd for permission to reproduce Figure 5 Programme Learning Curves taken from 'Community organizations and rural development: a learning process approach' by D.C. Korten in Public Administration Review 1980, pp.480–511.

This activity was supported by the Horizons programme and the International HIV/AIDS Alliance. Horizons conducts global operations research to improve HIV/AIDS prevention, care, and support programmes. Horizons is implemented by the Population Council in partnership with the International Center for Research on Women (ICRW), the Program for Appropriate Technology in Health (PATH), the International HIV/AIDS Alliance, Tulane University and Johns Hopkins University. Horizons is funded by the US Agency for International Development, under the terms of HRN-A-00-07-00012-00. The opinions expressed herein are those of the authors and do not necessarily reflect the views of the US Agency for International Development.

The Population Council is an international, non-profit, non-governmental institution that seeks to improve the well-being and reproductive health of current and future generations around the world and to help achieve a humane, equitable and sustainable balance between people and resources. The Council conducts biomedical, social science and public health research and helps build research capacities in developing countries. Established in 1952, the council is governed by an international board of trustees. Its New York headquarters supports a global network of regional and country offices.

The International HIV/AIDS Alliance is an international non-governmental organisation that supports communities in developing countries to prevent the spread of HIV, to support and care for those infected and to ease the impact of HIV on families and communities. Since its establishment in 1993, the Alliance has provided both financial and technical support to over 1500 HIV/AIDS projects and has worked with NGOs and CBOs from over 40 countries.

Foreword

Momentum for scaling up HIV/AIDS programmes and services has been steadily gaining ground in recent years. Alongside the inexorable spread of HIV, we are also witnessing growing determination by communities, NGOs, governments and other stakeholders that more must be done to address the devastating effects of the pandemic. In June 2001, a groundbreaking UN General Assembly Special Session on HIV/AIDS included the signing of a Declaration of Commitment by governments empowering stakeholders at the global, national and local levels to respond to HIV/AIDS with bold action. More recently the Global Fund to Fight AIDS, Tuberculosis and Malaria has been launched, with the aim of raising billions of dollars annually to combat these deadly diseases, in part through support of larger-scale and more concerted action. Even conservative lawmakers in the USA, who have long resisted increases in development assistance for HIV/AIDS, are now reversing their positions and calling for substantial new funding.

Although the new support and renewed attention are certainly welcome, it is clear that achieving larger-scale responses will require more than just additional resources. Scaling up NGO responses, the specific focus of this book, presents particular challenges and issues. While there seems to be a consensus about the importance of scaling up NGO programmes, there is less shared understanding of the contexts most conducive to scaling up, the type of NGO or NGO programme appropriate to expand, internal implications to scaling up, how to define and measure objectives, and how these processes depend on and interact with the political and social environment.

Participants at an Asia regional workshop organized by the International HIV/AIDS Alliance concluded that 'scale up is not a one-off, overnight event. It is a process that continues and is improved over time' (International HIV/AIDS Alliance, June 2001). There has also been recognition of the risks of attempting to scale up too quickly, either as a response to the urgency of the epidemic, pressure from donors or national governments, or community demands to respond.

Recognizing the need to draw together practical experiences of scaling up NGO HIV/AIDS programmes, the International HIV/AIDS Alliance and the Horizons programme, with financial support from the US Agency for International Development (USAID), initiated a project to identify lessons learned from the field of HIV/AIDS and other sectors that could help to guide NGO leaders, programme managers and policy makers as they seek to scale up. As part of this project, a literature review was produced (Eisele 2000) and a background paper was prepared to identify key concepts and lessons, including from other sectors that might be applicable to HIV/AIDS (DeJong 2000). A dozen case studies describing experiences with scaling up NGO work on HIV were also prepared (Horizons 2000). These documents provided the foundation for an international seminar convened in the UK in September 2000 to consolidate lessons to date, identify critical gaps in knowledge and articulate a research agenda for the future.

A richly diverse group of individuals and organizations participated in this project, including NGO and government representatives from Latin America, Africa and the Asia-Pacific; private and bilateral donors; UNAIDS; university academics; and development agency staff. All contributed invaluable ideas and expertise with impressive candour, and their willingness to share difficulties and failures as well as successes helped to enrich the process immeasurably.

The enthusiastic response from those who read the report synthesizing the background document, case studies and workshop outcomes, convinced us of the need to seek as wide a dissemination of our experiences as possible. To this end, we were delighted to consolidate our reflections and experience into this book, published by ITDG Publishing.

The various chapters outline with great clarity and 'real-life' examples the challenges and issues that typically confront NGO programmes as they seek to scale up. They help us to understand that scaling up involves so much more than just the need to increase coverage, and stimulate our thinking about how to ensure that our work in HIV/AIDS is of sufficient quality, what we can do to increase sustainability and how we can make sure our work is having an impact. We are also presented with a range of different strategies or options for scaling up beyond the usual approach of organizational expansion.

A common underlying message throughout the book is that although the issues and challenges to scaling up HIV/AIDS responses can seem formidable, there is no doubt that collectively we must make every effort to do so. Identifying the difficulties and sharing lessons from those who have grappled with scaling up before, as this book does, is an important step towards improving the overall response to HIV/AIDS, and making progress against an epidemic that has already caused so much suffering and loss of life.

Christopher Castle
Horizons programme, seconded from
the International HIV/AIDS Alliance

Acronyms

AMSED	Association Marocaine de Soldarité et Développement (Morocco)
ANCS	Association Nationale Contre le Sida (Senegal)
ASI	Asociacion de Salud Integral (Guatemala)
BCC	behaviour change communication
BRAC	Bangladesh Rural Advancement Committee
CBO	community-based organization
DFID	Department for International Development (UK)
FACT/FOCUS	Family AIDS Caring Trust/Family, Orphans and Children Under Stress (Zimbabwe)
FHT	Family Health Trust
HCNG	Home Care Network Group
HCT	home care team
HIV/AIDS	human immunodeficiency virus/acquired immune deficiency syndrome
KANCO	Kenya AIDS NGO Consortium
NACO	National AIDS Control Organization
NGO	non-governmental organization
PACT	Private Agencies Cooperating Together
PLHA	person/people living with HIV/AIDS
PSG	Project Support Group (Zimbabwe)
RFP	request for proposals
SIAAP	South India AIDS Action Programme
STI/STD	sexually transmitted infection/sexually transmitted disease
TASO	The AIDS Support Organization (Uganda)
UNAIDS	United Nations Programme on HIV/AIDS
UNICEF	United Nations Children's Fund
USAID	US Agency for International Development
VCT	voluntary counselling and testing
WHO	World Health Organization
YRGCare	YR Gaitonde Center for AIDS Research and Education (India)

Figures

Case Studies

PART I

BACKGROUND AND DEFINITIONS

CHAPTER ONE

The importance and urgency of scaling up HIV/AIDS responses

INTRODUCTION

It is now more than 20 years since the human immunodeficiency virus (HIV) was identified as the cause of acquired immune deficiency syndrome (AIDS). During these years, over 20 million people are estimated to have died because of the virus and a further 42 million men, women and children are currently living with HIV/AIDS (Figures 1 and 2).[1] HIV/AIDS is now the leading cause of death in sub-Saharan Africa and the fourth biggest killer in the world. The majority of people infected are young, sexually active adults, in or approaching the prime of life, often with dependent children and ageing parents. The effect of the epidemic has therefore been to leave millions of children without one or both parents, and huge numbers of elderly people have had to take on responsibility for multiple families of young children at a time of life when they should have expected support. In Africa, more than 12 million children have lost a mother or both parents. In some of the worst affected countries – currently in southern and eastern Africa where up to one-third of all children under 15 are estimated to have lost one or both parents – the alarming phenomenon of child-headed households is

	Total	Adults	Women	Children under 15
Number of people living with HIV/AIDS	42 000 000	38 600 000	19 200 000	3 200 000
People newly infected with HIV in 2001	5 000 000	4 200 000	2 000 000	800 000
AIDS deaths in 2001	3 100 000	2 500 000	1 200 000	610 000

Figure 1   Global summary of the HIV/AIDS epidemic as of end 2002
Source: UNAIDS December 2002 Epidemic Update.

TOTAL	42 000 000
Sub-Saharan Africa	29 400 000
South and South-east Asia	6 000 000
Latin America	1 500 000
East Asia and Pacific	1 200 000
Eastern Europe and Central Asia	1 200 000
North America	980 000
Western Europe	570 000
North Africa and Middle East	550 000
Caribbean	440 000
Australia and New Zealand	15 000

Figure 2 Adults and children estimated to be living with HIV/AIDS as of end 2002

Source: UNAIDS December 2002 Epidemic Update.

emerging. The overall effect on families, communities and societies where HIV/AIDS prevalence is high is likely to be catastrophic. Yet it is only in the past few years that there has been widespread recognition of the scale of the impact of HIV, or any global attempt to do anything significant about it.

Despite this health and humanitarian crisis, the programmes – whether run by national governments, the private sector, non-governmental organizations (NGOs) or international agencies – currently addressing this rapid and devastating spread of the pandemic clearly are not operating at sufficient scale or with enough impact to stem its progress. Thus there is an urgent moral dimension to the need to enlarge the scale of HIV/AIDS activities. Five million people were infected by the virus in 2002, and deaths from HIV will continue to rise over at least the next ten years. HIV/AIDS has spared no region of the world. Illustrating one of the greatest injustices and inequities of our era, the areas of the globe where 95% of those living with HIV reside, and which are experiencing the fastest and most relentless growth of the epidemic, are broadly defined as developing countries. These are the very countries that are least able to afford broad and equitable access to antiretroviral therapies against HIV/AIDS and treatments for opportunistic infections, or to provide care and support for those affected by it. In contrast, since 1996, people who are HIV-positive in rich countries have had access to antiretroviral drugs which – although they do not cure HIV/AIDS, may not be effective for all and have many side effects – can prolong the life of those with HIV.

People in developing countries are more susceptible to HIV/AIDS because of widespread poverty, inadequate social safety nets and social services, while at the same time, the social implications of HIV/AIDS are much more devastating than in the North. Widespread malnutrition weakens resistance to infection generally, and poverty and social alienation are the prime factors motivating risky sexual behaviour. Migrant workers – often young, single men – are particularly at risk of HIV as they join the ranks of the unemployed or poorly paid in urban peripheries. Civil unrest and violence, together with the accompanying social dislocation, exacerbate vulnerability to HIV infection. Many countries afflicted by HIV/AIDS are characterized by high levels of civil conflict or the breakdown of political systems and may be recovering from a prolonged struggle. In sub-Saharan Africa particularly, the type of conflict experienced has led to a breakdown in social mores, widespread sexual abuse (with rape sometimes used as a weapon of war) and demoralization – with significant implications for HIV (Epstein 2001). When these factors are combined with poor and declining health services in many countries, particularly in sub-Saharan Africa, there is a greater likelihood that sexually transmitted infections are left untreated, favouring the transmission of HIV. Poor levels of education in turn make it more difficult to reach people with health information.

Women are at particular risk of contracting HIV for both biological and social reasons. They represent approximately half of those infected with HIV/AIDS worldwide, yet in the worst affected region – sub-Saharan Africa – more women are infected than men. Redressing inequitable gender relations in terms of dealing with women's economic dependence on men, their lack of power in sexual relationships and their susceptibility to sexual abuse must be central to addressing the HIV/AIDS epidemic. The fact that in many developing countries women marry early, have less access to education than men, and social as well as labour norms value women mainly for their childbearing role means that their ability to negotiate 'safe sex' is limited. If infected, the social constraints and stigma are likely to be even greater for women than men, posing additional barriers to seeking such social support and care that is available.

At the same time, the broader implications of HIV/AIDS in poor countries are all the more devastating. As the epidemic robs families and communities of members of the working-age population, in a context marked by weak or non-existent social safety nets, large networks of dependents may lose economic support. Poverty is thus both a risk factor for HIV/AIDS and exacerbated by it. Inadequate legal protection means that employment discrimination against those with HIV is widespread, and inequitable property rights, particularly for women, deprive HIV/AIDS widows – or daughters – of inheritance.

In this dismal picture, some rays of light have begun to emerge as international attention has belatedly focused on the epidemic and its global inequities. Indeed, more than any disease before, HIV/AIDS is seen both as a global crisis that can only be addressed by the concerted action of world leaders and as a symbol of some of the social costs of unchecked globalization. Unprecedented international advocacy combining developing country governments and activists, NGOs (such as Oxfam and Medecins Sans Frontieres[2]) and consumer groups have demanded concessions from both multinational pharmaceutical corporations in drug pricing and in the very system of world trade regulation, the World Trade Organization. Breakthroughs at the 2001 World Trade Organization meeting in Doha mean that poor governments could modify patent rules which give such multinationals 20 years' patent protection[3] to allow local pharmaceutical manufacturers to produce generic versions of the patented drugs in the case of public health emergencies. These patent rules are the main cause of the non-affordability of such drugs in developing countries. While these trends have decreased the prices of antiretroviral drugs in developing countries to well below those in the North, access in the South still remains poor. Moreover, there are enormous constraints and complexities to the administration of such drugs in countries with weak and declining healthcare delivery capacity. Antiretroviral drugs themselves – although critical – are by no means a solution to the HIV/AIDS crisis in the developing countries.

The second positive result of the international focus on the HIV/AIDS epidemics has been the establishment of the Global Fund against AIDS, Tuberculosis and Malaria. The idea of creating an international funding mechanism to increase resources for these three global epidemics originated at the Okinawa G8 summit in July 2000. At the instigation of UN Secretary-General Kofi Annan and many national leaders, the concept of the Fund was unanimously endorsed in June 2001 at the UN General Assembly Special Session on HIV/AIDS. In July 2001, the G8 leaders meeting in Genoa committed US$1.3 billion to the Fund and further funding has been sought from international donors, the private sector and national governments. While pledges to date fall well below the target of $9 billion a year, and the actual disbursable funds for the first round of requests advertised in February 2002 were only $700 million, the Global Fund represents a huge step forward.[4] It also raises huge and controversial questions as to how this money should best be spent and contributes to pressures to scale up existing programmes on HIV/AIDS.

THE ROLE OF NON-GOVERNMENTAL ORGANIZATIONS IN HIV/AIDS

AIDS activities initiated by NGOs have had a disproportionate influence on the main ideas and strategies found within the HIV/AIDS sector. This is for a number of reasons, including the inherent advantages of the way NGOs tend to operate, as well as the fact that governments were often reluctant to respond to HIV/AIDS initially, or did so belatedly. From the early years of the epidemic, NGOs have pioneered new ways of responding to HIV/AIDS, and in some communities and settings have provided the only response to it. HIV is closely associated with sex and death, issues that are difficult to deal with through official governmental channels. In addition, HIV is linked to behaviours that are often illegal or socially unaccepted, such as drug use, homosexual behaviour or commercial sex work. While harm reduction approaches[5] are gradually being brought into some government policies, governments have found it difficult to appear to condone activities which are against their laws, and changing laws, of course, takes time and in many cases occurs only after prolonged efforts have been made at advocacy and persuasion. In some cases, governments have difficulty for political, economic or social reasons in even admitting that behaviours conducive to the spread of HIV/AIDS exist – a difficulty that is reinforced where societies are intolerant of such behaviours or lack good communication and education structures. Within these constraints, NGOs have been able to address the needs of stigmatized groups and behaviours at a more personal level, and have therefore been able to lead the way in finding paths to reach marginalized groups, who are likely to be most immediately and most severely affected by the epidemic.

NGOs are also able to respond quickly on a small scale, partly because they are not hampered by bureaucratic structures, and partly because they are often close to their constituencies and in a better position to understand the influences at a local level. Responses to HIV have therefore been characterized by a disproportionate role for

NGOs. NGO action, both on a community level, and through efforts at advocacy and policy analysis at the international and national levels, has often led the way in seeking equitable means of responding to the HIV/AIDS epidemic. Yet despite their decisive role and the proliferation of those working on HIV/AIDS, NGOs often experience particular difficulties in increasing the scale of their activities to reach larger numbers of people, to have an impact at levels higher than the 'community' and to address the broader social determinants of HIV/AIDS. Indeed, where NGOs have made pioneering contributions to public debate and approaches in the sector this has often been spontaneous, rather than a result of deliberate planning to increase the scale and impact of their activities.

ORIGINS AND STRUCTURE OF THE BOOK

Perceiving the urgent need for NGOs to expand the scale of their activities in the face of an escalating epidemic, Horizons and the International HIV/AIDS Alliance launched an initiative to examine the nature of the challenge to scale up in the context of HIV/AIDS internationally. This book was prepared as part of this initiative and addresses the specific challenge of deliberately increasing the scale of HIV/AIDS programmes run by NGOs in prevention, care and support programmes in developing countries. While the focus of the book is on the activities of NGOs, it recognizes that increasingly NGOs are engaging in partnerships with governments, academic institutions and other organizations in their quest to widen the impact of their activities. It asks whether there are lessons from the broader literature on development which are of relevance to HIV/AIDS. An initial draft was presented to an international seminar convened as part of this project at which 13 NGOs from around the world gave their own experience of scaling up.[6] The experiences and insights of these NGOs, each of which has engaged in a scaling-up process in some form, provide the basis of the findings of this book. They comprise a diversity of types of NGO, from small community-based organizations through national NGOs to international NGO support organizations. The case study organizations work in Latin America, Africa and Asia respectively, and in some cases in all three regions. Together they capture a variety of ways – although not the only ways – in which NGOs have responded to HIV/AIDS around the world. These include such activities as general prevention of the epidemic, or working with groups particularly vulnerable to HIV/AIDS, providing clinical services, drawing attention to the importance of counselling, engaging in advocacy and assisting small, local organizations in supporting orphans and communities affected by HIV. Examples of increasing the scale of NGO activities in HIV/AIDS given here draw primarily on these case studies, presentations and comments made at the seminar, and relevant available published documentation. Salient aspects of those NGO experiences are incorporated in case studies throughout the book.

This book is aimed at those active in the HIV/AIDS field who are interested in, or have a stake in increasing the impact of, NGO programmes. It is also directed towards those within the wider development field who are concerned about the impact of HV/AIDS and what NGOs can do about it. Chapter 10 addresses representatives of funding organizations active in HIV/AIDS and NGO support organizations. National AIDS programme managers may also find the book relevant, insofar as their work brings them into contact with a range of NGOs working on the epidemic. Finally, the book is aimed at students of development and public health who are concerned about HIV/AIDS.

The book is divided into three parts. The first provides a background to and definitions of the term 'scaling up' as used in development, and in Chapter 2 describes contrasting approaches to defining this term within the field of HIV/AIDS. Chapter 3 addresses some of the difficult choices that NGOs need to make in scaling up, such as that between maintaining quality and increasing coverage.

Part II focuses on strategic considerations for NGOs in thinking about scaling up. A typology of scaling-up processes relevant to HIV/AIDS is proposed in Chapter 4, drawing on existing experience of scaling up development programmes. Substantial attention is paid to some of the risks inherent in the scaling-up process as cautionary tales for those interested in embarking on it. Most of the strategies outlined in Chapter 4 entail some sort of partnership between the organization initiating scaling up and other types of institutions, and therefore Chapter 5 examines a range of types of partnership and both their difficulties and rewards. Chapter 6 then examines the importance of context and how such factors as the political and economic environment in which scaling up is planned as well as the level of the epidemic may influence choices of strategies for scaling up. It also analyses the varying motivations behind scaling up. In general, there is very little information or research on the costs of scaling up, an aspect that is of particular concern to NGOs, which are usually operating on a tight budget. Chapter 7 looks at how to approach the question of the cost of scaling up and what sort of costs might be incurred. Chapter 8 includes an analysis of the varied obstacles to scaling up programmes, both in general and how the sensitive nature of HIV/AIDS and diversity of contexts complicate the process.

Part III examines the institutional implications of scaling up and the many internal dimensions NGOs must take into consideration to prepare themselves for scaling up (Chapter 9). Chapter 10 is a discussion of the relevance of the arguments made here for both donors and NGO support organizations working in the field of HIV/AIDS. Part III ends with some general conclusions about the NGO experiences of scaling up documented in this book.

WHY SCALING UP IS IMPORTANT

The final quarter of the twentieth century witnessed a proliferation of NGOs working in social development (Edwards and Hulme 1992) and in health specifically (Gilson et al. 1994; Jareg and Kaseje 1998). Ironically, the role of NGOs was promoted both on the political left and right (Bratton 1989), and supported through donor assistance across the spectrum. On the one hand, NGOs were sought out by the political right as an avenue to circumvent the public sector, which was widely perceived to be slow in its response, bureaucratic and often corrupt. The advent of structural adjustment programmes calling for government cutbacks and a reduction in state-subsidized services paved the way for NGOs to fill the gaps left by the retreating state. At the same time, NGO expansion was also fuelled by sympathetic voices on the left. These argued that the participatory nature of NGOs, the fact that they represented the poor and marginalized, and their concern to address sensitive issues perpetuating underdevelopment and its attendant social problems made them a liberating influence on developing countries.

A more pragmatic argument for the contribution of NGOs has arisen with the recognition that in resource-poor settings where state capacity is weak, achieving broad national coverage in all areas of social development is beyond the capacities – and indeed sometimes the interests – of governments acting alone. This, as has been noted above, is particularly the case in HIV/AIDS.

This unchecked optimism has been somewhat moderated by a more sober assessment. While laudable, the impact of NGOs has often been limited in scale, fails to address the broader structural determinants of the problems of developing countries and does not translate into sustainable national programmes (Drabek 1987; Edwards and Hulme 1992). Moreover, there has been belated recognition that to achieve wider effect, in many cases NGOs need to abandon their staunch independence and forge better and more strategic links with government, despite the political difficulties in doing so on both sides of that relationship. NGOs, in this view, 'ignore government at their peril' (Edwards and Hulme 1992).

Thus, in development circles at least, there has been a growing chorus of voices calling for NGOs to increase the scale and impact of their activities and to build strategic alliances such that the effects of any one organization are multiplied and the pool of beneficiaries increases exponentially. Yet there has also been recognition that expansion may bring with it trade-offs – among them, between quality, quantity and costs, and between accountability to one's declared constituency and accountability to external funders financing the costs of expansion (e.g. Edwards and Hulme 1997; Pearce 1993). Thus, while a tentative consensus is emerging over the importance of scaling up, there is much less shared understanding of the contexts most conducive to scaling up; the types of organization or programme that it is most appropriate to expand; the relative costs of different types of programme; the internal implications of scaling up; how to define objectives; how to measure the impact of scaling up; and how these processes depend on and interact with the wider political and social environment.

THE URGENCY OF SCALING UP HIV/AIDS RESPONSES

The most convincing argument behind calls to expand the scale of activities in HIV/AIDS in developing countries is the moral and humanitarian one. Every day there are approximately 14 000 new HIV infections globally (UNAIDS 2002). Epidemiologically, the rapid transmission of HIV/AIDS can only be countered when prevention efforts are organized at sufficient scale to affect the dynamics of the epidemic. The demographics of the HIV/AIDS epidemic reveal the extent to which it is the working-age and younger generations that are disproportionately affected. Young people, who may lack access to correct information about the potential consequences of unsafe sexual behaviour, are particularly at risk of contracting sexually transmitted infections generally and HIV/AIDS specifically. More-over, internationally, more and more adolescents are having sexual relations before marriage, and the age at which first sexual inter-course occurs is decreasing (Smith and Colvin 2000). Adolescent women typically lack power over their sexual relations, yet epidemi-ological evidence from many parts of the world indicates a tendency for older men to seek sexual relations with younger and younger women, particularly as HIV prevalence rises and the latter are assumed not to be infected.

There is increasing frustration at the failure of many small-scale research, pilot or demonstration projects to get 'out of the hothouse' and have a larger influence on policies and programmes (Myers 1992: 370). This frustration is heightened in the area of HIV/AIDS as the epi-demic escalates. A World Bank report on HIV/AIDS in sub-Saharan Africa notes, for example, that among the lessons learned about suc-cessful HIV/AIDS prevention efforts is that small pilot programmes with no chance of duplication or replication are not helpful (World Bank 1999). In an article in *Science*, the director for rural development and environment at the World Bank (Binswanger 2000) gives a stark example of limited coverage in the Kagera Region of Tanzania where 200 000 of the region's 1.9 million people are children orphaned by AIDS. There, NGO directors stated that they operate mainly in two out of five districts, leaving three with almost no services, and in the two districts where they do work, they serve no more than an estimated 5% of the population.

Elsewhere, as a UNAIDS report states: '. . . action remains spo-radic and patchy rather than comprehensive. "Boutique"[7] projects may provide services for one or two communities, while large areas of the countryside have nothing. Many programmes have yet to become comprehensive in either geographical coverage or content' (UNAIDS 2000a: 109). Indeed, such is the lack of information about access and coverage that it is not generally known who has access to, let alone uses, HIV/AIDS-related services. Estimates of current levels of coverage in sub-Saharan Africa for HIV/AIDS prevention interventions suggest that overall coverage is less than 20% of the target populations in most countries (Kumaranayake and Watts 2000a). Currently, only a small proportion of people living with HIV and AIDS have access to home care services, and home care needs are growing five to ten times faster than the availability of home care, meaning that coverage figures are likely to fall even further (Nsutebu et al. 2001).

Clearly the onus is now on those working in HIV/AIDS – including funding organizations – to explore the question of increasing scale and to make efforts, fully cognisant of the risks involved, to identify what programmes or which aspects of their programmes can be scaled up. This responsibility falls on all those whose work touches on HIV/AIDS, not only NGOs, although the focus of this book is on the latter. While there may be consensus on the need to scale up, there is less agreement over the objectives and the most appropriate approaches to scaling up, as will be addressed in the next section.

WHAT IS MEANT BY 'SCALING UP'?

Considerable confusion surrounds the various terms used to refer to expansion of the scale of activities, whether 'going to scale', 'scaling up' or 'widening impact'. The word 'scale' is both a relative and an absolute concept (Myers 1992), and thus may indicate on the one hand reaching a greater number of people or, on the other hand, a notion of a particular size of population, activity or particular measure of interest. The actual unit of measurement is also a source of confusion. In the development literature, 'scale' has been used to refer to what could be described as both the 'input' and the 'output' aspects of scaling up – that is, on the one hand to organizational size or type of activity engaged in, and on the other to 'outputs' such as scale of coverage of people or geographic area (see Figure 3). Even within the concept of coverage there is a difference between coverage of absolute numbers of people, and coverage as expressing a percentage of a total population or particular groups (Myers 1992).

Looking at the range of processes that are relevant to HIV/AIDS, it is clear that scaling up may simply entail increasing the size or level of activity of a particular organization. As used in the development literature (e.g. Edwards and Hulme 1992), the term has also been used to imply enlarging the scope of the activities of an organization in order to reach more people. For example, an organization focusing on HIV/AIDS prevention and awareness raising may move into support and care for people with HIV/AIDS as the epidemic progresses and prevalence rises. In 1992, Edwards and Hulme made a distinction between integrating other horizontal activities – that is unrelated activities, as opposed to vertical activities that deal with the same problem. For example, an organization providing micro-credit might diversify horizontally to provide health services, or vertically to

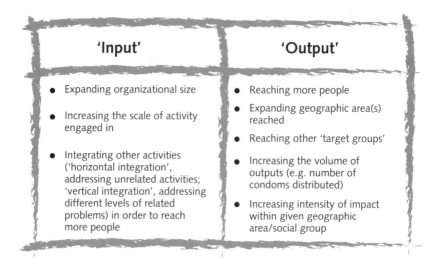

'Input'	'Output'
• Expanding organizational size	• Reaching more people
• Increasing the scale of activity engaged in	• Expanding geographic area(s) reached
	• Reaching other 'target groups'
• Integrating other activities ('horizontal integration', addressing unrelated activities; 'vertical integration', addressing different levels of related problems) in order to reach more people	• Increasing the volume of outputs (e.g. number of condoms distributed)
	• Increasing intensity of impact within given geographic area/social group

Figure 3   Various definitions of scaling up used in the development literature

develop programmes addressing high default rates on repayment. An example of horizontal integration of HIV/AIDS work into income-generation work has occurred in Morocco, where the Association Marocaine de Soldarité et Devéloppement (AMSED) has scaled up its work on HIV/AIDS by reaching out to the micro-credit community which, in Morocco, is already well mobilized.

On the 'output' side, scaling up may entail increasing the absolute numbers of people reached, or it could include expansion to other geographic areas (regions or countries), whether by opening new branches or linking with other organizations. An organization may also diversify the range of social groups with which it interacts. Economists in particular may measure scaling up simply by the volume of outputs of activities, such as the number of condoms provided or distributed (Kumaranayake 2000). Finally, scaling up has been used less frequently in the development literature to mean intensifying effort within a particular social group, population or geographic area in order to increase impact.

Drawing on prevailing definitions of 'scaling up' in the development literature more broadly, Chapter 4 discusses a number of strategies used by NGOs to scale up their HIV/AIDS efforts. These encompass both the 'input' and 'output' aspects of scaling up, and denote the process of expanding the scale of activities with the ultimate objective of increasing the numbers of people reached and the impact on the problem at hand. As Myers (1992) reminds us, a preoccupation with increasing scale can distract us from the actual objective of scaling up, which in this case is to reduce the spread or to alleviate the effects of the epidemic. A programme that increases its scale may well lose in terms of its impact (Edwards and Hulme 1992) as the intensity of effort is necessarily reduced. In HIV/AIDS, for instance, a larger organization may no longer be able to provide the personalized education and care of a small organization and as a result will be less effective. Thus the goal of increasing coverage is clearly insufficient in and of itself. The relationships between coverage, impact, cost and quality are dynamic, and change according to both the level of the epidemic and the objectives of the scaling up. These dimensions of scaling up are addressed in the context of HIV/AIDS in Chapter 2.

CHAPTER TWO

Defining scaling up in the context of HIV/AIDS: different perspectives

TOP DOWN VERSUS BOTTOM UP: A QUESTION OF VANTAGE

As we have seen in Chapter 1, there is little consensus on the definition of scaling up in development in general. Given the sensitive nature of HIV/AIDS and the variety of different perspectives from which it is approached, agreement on what precisely is meant by scaling up becomes even more difficult to achieve.

More so than in most development matters, debates over the appropriate approach to the epidemic are heated. In most developing countries, HIV/AIDS is still a fatal disease. Prevention of HIV/AIDS requires behavioural change in the most intimate aspects of human experience, and adequate care and support is premised not only on the availability and accessibility of appropriate services but also on breaking down entrenched social prejudices. While it is argued by some that the devastation brought about by the rapidly spreading epidemic calls for strong, centralized or top-down measures, others counter that such HIV/AIDS interventions run a high risk of creating ethical and human rights violations, and that effective interventions need to be based on strengthening people's responses to the epidemic. Early approaches to programmes in both developed and developing countries have shown that where interventions focus exclusively on so-called 'core transmitters' (or those groups that epidemiologically speaking are most at risk of HIV/AIDS and of transmitting it to the general population) without sensitivity to the ethical and human rights implications, they only further stigmatize these groups and thus may undermine both prevention and care efforts.[8]

Both those who argue for a centralized approach at the national level to deliver large-scale interventions, and those who focus more on working at a community level to motivate behavioural change and support those affected by HIV/AIDS, would agree on the fact that high-level political commitment to addressing HIV/AIDS is critical. Differences in approach emerge, in that the latter would attach more importance than the former to ensuring that individuals and communities have the information, tools and ultimately power to reduce their vulnerability. This somewhat exaggerated dichotomy also reflects differences in the broader health arena as to whether one adopts a medical or social model of health (Evans 1999). A medical model would assume that programmes should focus on particular interventions or using technologies that are known to affect the limited range of specific behaviours that have an impact on the evolution of the epidemic. By contrast, the social model of health would focus more on the broader social determinants of the health problems concerned.

In the case of HIV/AIDS, therefore, a social approach would entail addressing the social processes and inequalities that drive the epidemic and intensify its effects. For example, structural changes in gender inequalities and in the differential power in sexual negotiation between men and women and the elimination of sexual coercion are critical in reducing vulnerability to HIV transmission. This approach would argue that without greater control by people over the circumstances governing their health-related behaviour, long-term vulnerability to the epidemic would not be addressed. In practice, many NGOs active in HIV/AIDS may derive elements of their programmes from both perspectives, but in general the social model is likely to predominate.[9]

Following from these debates, approaches to scaling up and the question of impact depend on whether one adopts a national or community perspective, a public health/epidemiological or developmental approach. They also depend on whether one is referring to prevention or caring for, supporting and improving the quality of life of those infected by HIV, although, as discussed in more detail later in this chapter, there are strong synergies between prevention and care. National governmental authorities generally want to reach a scale that represents a significant proportion of a given country's population. They would share with those supporting a public health/ epidemiological perspective a major concern in preventing the epidemic, and therefore in reaching a sufficient scale to have an impact on the evolution of the epidemic. While care and support for those infected and affected by HIV may also be a national priority, governments typically give priority to prevention over care and support until a relatively high proportion of the population is infected.[10] Similarly, economists (whose perspective is presented in more detail in Chapter 7) would analyse scale in terms of the coverage reached or impact attained in relation to a finite level of resources – a concern about the best and most efficient use of resources often shared by cash-strapped developing country governments as well as by international donors. A World Bank paper on costing HIV/AIDS scaling up articulates this concern: 'How can we reach the greatest number in the cheapest manner?' (World Bank 2000).

To those subscribing to economistic or governmental perspectives, therefore, 'scale' is likely to denote an absolute level of coverage (usually of services or interventions) in order to have impact (usually defined in terms of spread of the epidemic). By contrast, a community-based or non-governmental organization might share the above long-term goals but be more immediately concerned about changing the underlying social parameters in which HIV/AIDS activities are carried out. Examples here would include reducing the stigma associated with the disease, passing legislation which makes discrimination against those with HIV/AIDS less likely or helping households and communities to cope when their members are hit by HIV/AIDS. Impact in these cases is clearly difficult – although not impossible – to measure. This notion of scaling up is likely to be a more relativistic one, where progress is evaluated in relation to the capacity of a given organization, the level of need among the population that organization is aiming to reach or the nature of social trends it is confronting. While many may focus on services or interventions, their emphasis lies more on the process of engaging their respective constituents and eliciting a response, a component of which is likely to be greater demand for services.

According to a social model of health, the need to scale up may focus on inducing long-term social change that would enable societies or particular communities to come to terms with the HIV/AIDS epidemic[11]. An individual is more likely to change behaviour if those around him or her – and particularly peers in similar social contexts – are also changing (Hughes 1993). Thus change on a collective level acts to reduce the risk factors conducive to the spread of HIV between individuals. The basis of behavioural change lies deeper within the norms and values perpetuated by society across generations. Modifying expectations, beliefs and attitudes at a societal level is necessary in the long term for sustained change in HIV-related behaviour to become the norm.

Such changes are only likely to come about and be sustained when there is corresponding progress in the policy and legislative context underpinning HIV/AIDS efforts. This, in turn, is most often induced when there is sufficient public debate and civic engagement concerning HIV/AIDS to put pressure on governmental bodies to demand response. Thus the issue of scale becomes a prerequisite for broader change. In many cases, groups disproportionately affected by the epidemic have brought about such pressures through community organizing at a local level. Such groups often lack political power individually, but are able to have an impact collectively. The organization of gay groups in the US is of course a classic example. Yet at the same time, activism based on identity politics can also have its dangers in impeding efforts to expand interventions more broadly so that they permeate the whole society. As Richard Parker has argued: 'The very effectiveness of local-level politics has made it difficult to build a broader coalition to address HIV/AIDS as a global issue and the kinds of social movements that have emerged around other (similarly global) issues such as environment, or reproductive health and rights' (Parker 2000: 48). That said, the 1990s witnessed the rise of global movements around HIV/AIDS as the disease has come to be seen as a symbol of the social costs of unconstrained globalization. The policies of multinational corporations and the World Trade Organization regarding access to antiretroviral therapies have been more closely scrutinized. As noted above, this has resulted in some breakthroughs concerning accessibility of such drugs in the developing world, and has greatly increased international attention to HIV/AIDS.

Disparities of definitions of scaling up, therefore, reflect more than semantics but rather result from underlying differences in philosophy, approach and objectives. NGOs, although they vary enormously in initial size, largely share the local or community perspective outlined above. That is, the process of scaling up at the micro or community level is given more attention than reaching a specific level of scale in terms of the epidemiological picture at the national level. Emphasis is placed on the social change needed to both prevent HIV/AIDS and improve the lives of those affected by it. At the same time, NGOs are also influenced by prevailing knowledge about what interventions are effective in countering HIV/AIDS and retain a focus on producing an impact on the epidemic.

Not all NGOs start from a similar initial scale of activity or the same micro-level frame of reference. Indeed, the examples given in this book range from small community-based operations (such as that by Family AIDS Caring Trust/Family, Orphans and Children Under Stress (FACT/FOCUS) in Zimbabwe – Case Study 10), to national (such as the

Kenya AIDS NGO Consortium (KANCO) – Case Study 12), to regional (such as the Project Support Group in Zimbabwe (PSG) – Case Study 1) and even to international initiatives led by NGOs (such as Private Agencies Co-operating Together (PACT) – Case Study 7; or the International HIV/AIDS Alliance – Case Study 11). Moreover, many NGOs, particularly those that assume a 'catalysing role' in supporting smaller organisations technically and/or financially (see Strategy 2 in Chapter 4), may begin with a national frame of reference. And NGOs acting together can clearly combine to create a national force, as is the case with the national coalition of HIV/AIDS organizations comprised by KANCO (Kenya), which does not operate local field offices. Indeed, Myers' term 'association' (see Chapter 4), which he argued might be particularly useful in the field of early childhood education, may similarly be an effective strategy in HIV/AIDS. He uses the term to mean expanding programme size through common efforts and alliances among a group of organizations, each of which develops similar programmes but tailors them to the needs of specific communities or populations.

Whatever the discrepancies in starting points and definitions of scaling up, there is a consensus and a shared concern that the ultimate objective of scaling up initiatives is to have greater impact on preventing the epidemic and mitigating its effects. Moreover, all perspectives recognize that scaling up needs to be sustainable, not only in financial terms but according to a number of other criteria, including whether it is technically sound and can be supported both politically and socially (discussed more fully below). Again, there may be differences in how both these dimensions of scaling up are expressed and measured, as the following section makes clear.

GAUGING IMPACT

To categorize the concerns of NGOs in scaling up as being a relative notion of scaling up as opposed to an absolute one is not to release NGOs from the need to demonstrate impact. The founder of the Project Support Group in Zimbabwe, which began as a university research department and pays careful attention to monitoring the impact of their programmes on measurable outcomes such as condom use, notes that: 'Process cannot be a substitute for structure or results'.

Measuring the impact of interventions in the HIV/AIDS context is more challenging than is the case with many other health problems.

HIV/AIDS differs from many other health problems for which intervention efforts have been scaled up, such as disability or diarrhoeal disease. Efforts to increase the use of oral rehydration therapies for the treatment of diarrhoea, for example, have succeeded in reaching a large scale in many developing countries. Yet the behavioural change implied, though affected by socio-economic context, is not as conditioned by social and gender power relations as is condom use, for example. And, unlike the area of early childhood care, where Myers recommends focusing the scaling-up effort on those 'at risk', defining such a population in HIV/AIDS may be difficult given the lack of knowledge about sexual behaviour. There is also a danger that it may lead to stigmatizing that group. In the worst case, singling out certain social groups for intervention may lead to abuse of ethical and human rights principles.

By contrast, HIV/AIDS is distinctive in its mutually reinforcing relationship between prevention and care. Indeed, as the UNAIDS (2000a) report on the global AIDS epidemic reports, not only will sick individuals benefit from care and support, but prevention efforts will be credible and effective only if they are matched by humane and high-quality care and support services. Prevention messages which rely on inducing fear or shame as a means to alerting people to HIV, without also including messages of support for those who are affected, will lead to stigmatization and discrimination, as those affected will be labelled, or will label themselves, as either immoral or careless. The fear of stigmatization and the resulting discrimination this engenders will mean that people who think they may have HIV will be reluctant to seek testing, and those who know their status may be discouraged from seeking help and treatment. It is important that this is countered so that people with HIV are freely able to access the information and technologies that will help to prevent transmission of the virus to others.

Thus while targeted interventions are critical to limit the spread of the epidemic, sensitivity to social prejudices and HIV-associated stigma needs to be foremost among the concerns of those engaged in planning the intervention concerned. As Jeff O'Malley of the International HIV/AIDS Alliance stated: 'A key lesson from the Alliance's programming experience has been the importance of paying attention to key populations that affect epidemic dynamics, especially in low prevalence countries with concentrated epidemics. However, this does not mean ignoring other populations, since one community affects another's choices and options. Scaling up involves providing both intensive services and programmes for key populations, while working more cheaply with broader communities to raise awareness, challenge stigma and to ensure referrals when appropriate to more intensive efforts' (International HIV/AIDS Alliance and GlaxoSmithKline 2001: 21).

One example of a sensitive public health issue that has been scaled up in a number of contexts and has many parallels to HIV/AIDS is that of post-abortion care. Post-abortion care can be defined as including treatment of complications resulting from the abortion, provision of family planning services and linkages to other reproductive health services (Julie Solo, Reproductive Health Alliance). It represents a similar challenge to scaling up HIV/AIDS in its sensitivity and the need to address cultural norms and attitudes in order to expand the scale of this service. In this case, scaling up is defined as reaching a greater number of people and increasing the impact of the intervention with a specific objective of regularizing it into routine public sector health services. A comparative analysis of the successes and failures of such scaling-up efforts was made across four countries (Kenya, Ghana, Mexico and Colombia) and found that where efforts focused too much on the technology and not enough on changing social attitudes, scaling up was less successful. Scaling up was most successful where there was an understanding of the implications for essential systems and standards, such as supervision, and where there was both committed leadership and sufficient support for the intervention among the general public as opposed to among health personnel exclusively.

There are a number of specific challenges in finding measures of evaluating the impact of scaling up in HIV/AIDS. First, as elaborated above, the objective of organizations in scaling up their programmes may not only be an epidemiological one, as measured by incidence of new cases of HIV/AIDS. Rather, they often seek social changes – affecting social norms or reducing prejudice and stigma associated with HIV/AIDS – which are very difficult to measure and assessments of which tend to be qualitative and highly subjective. Quantitative indicators may not reflect the quality of effort the organization undertakes, particularly at the level of person-to-person contact, nor would they be sufficient to assess how well objectives of reducing stigma and discrimination are met, or how humane the care and support services are. Thus measuring the impact of NGO programmes on the epidemic cannot solely be measured by a reduced incidence of HIV/AIDS. Qualitative indicators relating to processes such as reduction of discrimination and changes in attitudes are also relevant.

Many NGOs addressing HIV/AIDS lack baseline data on which to evaluate the effectiveness of their scaling up. This may be due, at least in part, to a lack of research capacity or an institutional culture favouring the collection and analysis of data, as the example from SIAAP shows (see Case Study 5). NGOs may also lack the technological capacity to obtain the data. As Margarita Quevedo of KIMIRINA notes about Ecuador, for example, while epidemiological information on HIV/AIDS is available on the Internet, most of the small community-based organizations with which her organization works lack computers. In some cases, baseline data are not collected simply because NGOs are created to address a new and urgent need and, in their commitment to addressing this, research is not a priority in the early stages. Even where epidemiological information is available, for example, reliable and valid sexual behaviour data are often extremely difficult to obtain or collect for both cultural and political reasons. Where sexual behaviour studies have been conducted, such data – and particularly projections based on them – have to be scrutinized carefully for potential biases.

In real life, programmatic choices are often made without being fully informed by empirical data about impact. This is a controversial area for NGOs – while there is consensus that the ideal is to evaluate a programme or project before scaling it up, there is still extensive discussion relating to the difficulty of doing so.

SUSTAINING WHAT?

A further dimension to scaling up is that of sustainability. That is, the expansion of activities – whether in terms of people, geographic area, social group or activity – has to be built with sufficient financial, technical, social and political support so that it lasts over time.

The most frequent use of the term 'sustainability' refers to whether or not there are sufficiently strong economic bases to keep a given programme effective over a period of time. HIV/AIDS-related organizations, as is the case in many other areas of development, are often deficient in not taking the cost implications of alternative strategies into full consideration. There is an urgent need for more information on costing HIV/AIDS programmes (Kumaranayake and Watts 2000b).[12]

A broader understanding of sustainability would embrace a much fuller range of dimensions. Avina, in an article on the evolutionary cycles of NGOs, defines sustainability as follows: 'An expansion is successful if the organisation has evolved institutionally to the point where it can manage the augmented level of activities effectively, can finance itself into the foreseeable future, has retained the necessary level of programme autonomy from external actors and is providing desired and sustainable services to its target beneficiaries' (Avina 1993: 465–66). Both programmatic sustainability and organizational sustainability need to be considered: has the organization accumulated sufficient programme experience and momentum to operate on a larger scale? And does the organization have in place the requisite trained staff, processes and structures to sustain a greater level of activity to meet the objectives of a scaled-up programme? Indeed, the process of increasing the scale of activity may in itself reduce sustainability as the organization becomes overstretched and programme effectiveness is diluted. Thus it is critical that a thorough assessment of the capacity of the organization to scale up is made prior to engaging in the exercise (this is the focus of Part III).

The above dimensions of sustainability focus more on the organization itself and its supply or delivery of services. But the objectives of scaling up may be more than sustaining any particular programme or intervention in delivery terms. In many cases, it will relate more to sustaining the response of communities and the relevant constituencies of the organization to the epidemic, particularly in terms of sustained behavioural change. According to Geoff Foster, one of the key lessons that emerged from FACT/FOCUS support to community-led orphan support programmes in Zimbabwe (described further in Case Study 10) was the degree to which community ownership made the project more sustainable. Foster argues convincingly that African countries affected by HIV/AIDS have responded to the epidemic on their own terms in a number of ways, yet initiatives of external agencies – whether NGOs, governments or donors – often fail to recognize these community initiatives or, in the worst cases, disregard or undermine them.[13]

Thus sustainability in its broadest sense focuses on strengthening local initiatives and sustaining community ownership over programmes. Several NGOs described in this book (for example, Family Health Trust Anti-AIDS Clubs, the Salvation Army and FACT/FOCUS) see their role as catalysing and strengthening existing community initiatives, rather than bringing programmes to communities. All these programmes then seek to help communities themselves transfer the experience to other communities (or, in the case of the Anti-AIDS

Clubs in Zambia, to other schools). This is different from seeing the NGO itself as the driving force that 'delivers' interventions. In this sense, the social context in which the programme expands its scale of activities influences its sustainability. At the same time, outside agencies may need to encourage communities to recognize issues that are hidden or controversial, or to address social groups at the margins of society. It is possible that increased local responses to HIV/AIDS generate demand by breaking down social barriers and reducing stigma. In this sense, a 'virtuous cycle' could be created where increased coverage generates more demand or further local responses and thus the programme in question becomes more effective.

SCALING UP AS A PROCESS

The comparative advantage of NGOs in general lies more in the quality of their relationships than in the size of the resources they command, according to Fowler (1991). In HIV/AIDS, the great strengths of NGO activity to date have been the relationships of trust they have inspired among their constituencies and the processes of participatory decision-making they encourage, both of which have enabled them to address sensitive issues. Therefore, although it is important to be clear about the end objectives of scaling up, one also needs to recognize that the process of reaching these aims is significant both programmatically and for the organization involved.

Approaches to the process of scaling up expounded by the private sector, such as franchising and developing particular pilot models of which exact replicas are planted in starkly different contexts, have been very influential in development circles (Wazir and van Oudenhoven 1998). Yet they may not be appropriate strategies for the field of HIV/AIDS, where the importance of factoring in local specificities and the need for attention to processes and values is pre-eminent. As Myers notes, the challenge is to think about scale in a way that 'allows a qualitative, decentralised and participatory approach to that goal, as contrasted with the more quantitative, centralised and imposed approach that seems to predominate' (Myers 1992). Nonetheless, the opposite extreme of arguing that programmes are so context-specific as to make lessons or replication to other areas impossible, an approach that Wazir and van Oudenhoven (1998) refer to as 'contextualist', is also unhelpful. There is much that can be learned from small-scale efforts that is of larger relevance and applicability.

Examples of successful scaling-up efforts of HIV/AIDS NGOs with clear impact suggest that some degree of distinctiveness and integrity of process needs to be sacrificed in the interest of reaching a greater scale. Both the Project Support Group (PSG) in Zimbabwe and The AIDS Support Organization (TASO) in Uganda, for instance, illustrate that the development of standardized approaches with enough flexibility to allow for diversity among different communities can be highly effective. The prevention and mitigation efforts of the PSG share a common approach by training community volunteers through the use of modules, manuals and structured participatory approaches. As they describe it: '[Both prevention and mitigation] work with community volunteers to deliver large-scale, economical, locally relevant services that increase community response capacity' (see Case Study 1). The organization is exceptional in its rigorous attention to results. In one area, for example, they were able to demonstrate that Bulawayo condom use in sex work rose from 18% at outset to 72% within 2 years. While, particularly at the beginning, early partnerships 'resent the loss of attention and uniqueness as scaling up proceeds', resistance seems to wane as clear indications of the success of this approach emerge. PSG has grown from a small-scale effort based on a research project to a regional organization operating in three Southern African countries.

Similarly, TASO helps local community-based organizations to develop counselling and clinical services for those with HIV/AIDS, thus leading to a proliferation of 'TASO-like' services, each of which is tailored to specific communities (see Case Study 8). Thus TASO has identified a particular approach which it has tried to expand in a somewhat standardized manner to a wide geographic area, but at the same time allowing for flexibility to local circumstances.

If scaling up is conceived as a process occurring over time, objectives of the exercise may vary according to, for example, the different stages or level of the epidemic. At low levels of epidemic, when infection may be more restricted to certain social groups, different strategies may be called for than when the epidemic is more generalized within the population at large. At this stage, more 'targeted' interventions can prevent the spread of HIV into the 'general' population. Where HIV/AIDS is widespread, there needs to be a relatively high level of coverage within the general population in order to have the same degree of impact (although an incremental increase in coverage may have a significant relative impact). This is illustrated further in

Case Study 1 Project Support Group (Zimbabwe). The importance of evaluation

The Project Support Group (PSG) is a regional NGO that evolved from the University of Zimbabwe as a service delivery institution with the aim of complementing the university's research activities on HIV/AIDS and sexually transmitted infections (STIs). Originating in a university, it has paid careful attention since its inception to measuring the impact of its intervention on sexual behaviour change, and is exemplary in that regard. In 1987, women who participated in an ethnographic study of HIV initiated by the University in Bulawayo, Zimbabwe's second largest city, requested STI and HIV/AIDS education and services, which the Council of that city agreed to provide. With the University of Zimbabwe's support, other health authorities and community organizations in Zimbabwe followed the Bulawayo City Council's lead, developing projects for HIV-vulnerable communities of women and men.

As the demand for its assistance grew with an escalating number of partners, PSG became increasingly formalized and changed its status to a regional non-profit organization with a regional governance structure. It now operates in eight Southern African countries that are among the highest HIV prevalence countries in the world (Zimbabwe, Zambia, South Africa, Malawi, Botswana, Swaziland, Lesotho and Mozambique). As it expanded its scale of activities, PSG recruited additional staff and formed an associate group of 20 experienced field coordinators to provide training and support to regional partners. Rigorous evaluation was always conducted prior to further expansion.

PSG's approach to scaling up has focused on training and supporting local community volunteers to deliver services rather than expansion of its own organization. From the beginning, it recognized the need for highly structured, standardized approaches in order to reach a sufficient scale to have an impact on the evolution of the epidemic and to mitigate its effects. Staff belonging to the organization have developed modules and manuals and used structured participatory approaches to training, which are adapted according to local circumstances. The organization aims to increase the capacity of communities to respond to the epidemic. Before expanding into new countries, PSG consults with beneficiaries on expansion plans and uses the latter's insights to identify sites and strategies most appropriate in those settings.

In prevention, volunteers serve as peer educators, providing training, and encouraging behavioural change and condom use particularly in low-income, HIV-vulnerable communities. For example, in Mutare,

Zimbabwe, community peer educators organize thousands of community meetings, reaching men in workplaces, bars and nightclubs, and women in homes and markets. Staff members use participatory approaches to stimulate community debate and to shape safer sexual norms. They give low-income women STI treatment cards to enable them to gain access to free, high-quality treatment.

To mitigate the effects of the epidemic, volunteers work as providers of care, and support community members to care for family members with HIV and orphans. For example, in Masoyi, South Africa, staff train church members who have volunteered to serve as care providers in palliative care and, once trained, they visit the families to provide care and support, assist the families and, in turn, train the families to provide high-quality palliative care.

PSG uses research to inform its scaling-up strategies, both in terms of designing programmes and in evaluating their effects. Studies currently underway are addressing topics such as alternative approaches to reducing STI/HIV transmission among HIV-vulnerable adults, and evaluating the coverage, economy and quality of community AIDS care. For example, through community coverage surveys, it was learned that in Bulawayo, 80% of 705 sex workers attended peer education meetings and 91% of these received condoms during meetings. The research effort, however, went further to ascertain whether high coverage also translated into behavioural change and whether the behavioural change was indeed related to the intervention.

Condom use in sex work rose from 18% at the beginning of the programme to 72% within two years. Moreover, condom use in the last commercial sex act was reported by 27% of those who had attended no meetings, 46% of those who had attended one meeting and 77% of those who had attended two or more meetings. In turn, behaviour change appears to have contributed to reduce STI rates: in Zimbabwe project sites, these rates fell by 48% in Bulawayo, 52% in Mutare and 74% in Masvingo. Such findings have been validated through independent evaluations by international universities in the UK and the USA. Thus PSG has concrete evidence of the effectiveness of its approaches.

From its own perspective, PSG faced difficulties in preventing the expansion from diluting quality, including research quality, particularly in those sites with no research expertise, and building country support mechanisms in each country. Unlike many organizations, however, they have concrete data to measure changes in quality. In general, the scaling up improved morale because staff and volunteers felt part of an evolving organization with an expanded and clearly demonstrated impact.

Figure 4. Thus, as discussed below, the target groups of programmes are likely to change over time.

Modifying the objectives of programmes as scaling up proceeds may also be necessitated by changes in the political context. For example, the International HIV/AIDS Alliance adapted its strategy because the international donor landscape changed, and in India, the course of the scaling up of the Healthy Highways project to reduce transmission among truck workers and their sexual partners was affected both by policy changes within the main funding organization, the UK Department for International Development, and the desire of the Government of India to command greater direction over HIV/AIDS activities. These are two examples of ways in which NGOs have found it important to be able to respond to unanticipated changes in the policy environment during the scaling-up process.

Objectives of scaling up might also change over time due to the internal situation of the organization. At some stages in the scaling-up process it may be necessary to cut back in order to strengthen programmes and prepare for expansion – thus an organization may initially need to scale down in order to scale up.[14] It is not clear whether this is typical of NGO experiences of scaling up.

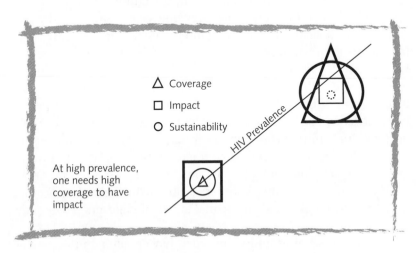

Figure 4   The relationship between coverage and impact according to level of HIV prevalence

Source: From a group exercise at the Horizons/Alliance Seminar (September 2000).

A DYNAMIC RELATIONSHIP BETWEEN PREVENTION, CARE AND MITIGATION

HIV/AIDS is distinctive among health problems in the dynamic relationship between preventing its incidence and supporting, caring for and treating those infected and affected by it. If the premise of scaling-up initiatives is to build the capacity of individuals and communities to respond to the epidemic, many would argue that the starting point should be problems identified by the constituencies with which NGOs work. In many contexts, such community initiatives are more likely to emerge to care for and support those affected by HIV/AIDS, such as in the area of orphan support. Children may often represent those most visibly affected by the epidemic towards whom humanitarian efforts are readily addressed. There is often more resistance to working with marginalized social groups who may be subject to prejudiced views that they are somehow 'morally responsible' for the epidemic. Similarly, communities typically avoid sensitive issues pertaining to gender-based violence.

Thus, although care may provide the catalyst for a broader approach to HIV/AIDS, scaling up prevention programmes may require more external motivation than that of care programmes. For example, church-based programmes across Africa have emerged to care for orphans and support families affected by the epidemic, but they may find prevention messages addressing condoms and sexual behaviour more problematic. Similarly, scaling up orphan support programmes, such as that initiated by FACT/FOCUS (Zimbabwe), not only reaches a larger number of orphans and vulnerable children, but there may be further, less obvious and difficult-to-measure benefits which illustrate the links between care, mitigation and prevention in HIV/AIDS. As Foster notes: 'Community ownership of orphan support programmes may reduce discrimination and encourage supportive actions towards orphan households [and] . . . the knowledge that there is an organisation in the community concerned about the welfare of orphans may lead to less physical and sexual abuse of children' (Foster et al. 1996: 401).

In some cases, community initiatives have emerged in the area of prevention and have subsequently moved into care. For example, the Anti-AIDS Clubs, which the Family Health Trust has supported in Zambia, moved from awareness raising and prevention in schools to working with orphans. In the words of Dixter Kaluba of the Family

Health Trust (Zambia), this has helped to familiarize youth with problems associated with the epidemic and thus 'young people don't feel the epidemic is so distant'. Elsewhere, in low-prevalence settings, where HIV/AIDS is not visible to the majority of community members, it may be easier to stimulate community participation in prevention rather than care.[15]

In Cambodia, a home-based care programme has provided a critical link between care, prevention and mitigating the effects of the epidemic. Cambodia has one of the fastest-growing HIV/AIDS epidemics in the world, yet faces a severe shortage of hospital beds. It has a poor population, only a minority of which can pay for prophylactic drug therapies, and a high incidence of people with symptomatic HIV infection and opportunistic infections (Wilkinson et al. 2000). Community leaders in Phnom Penh told an evaluation team, for example, that until the Home Care Team started visiting, people did not believe there was AIDS in their areas. Their visits helped to increase knowledge about HIV/AIDS and engendered an understanding of preventive measures (Wilkinson et al. 2000) (see Case Study 9).

Despite the evident synergies elaborated above in scaling up prevention, care and mitigation efforts, in many contexts, interventions in these areas may compete for resources. A World Bank report on costing the expansion of HIV/AIDS programmes in Africa notes, for example, that as HIV prevalence rises there are increasing costs associated with the burden of care. Therefore there will be greater tensions in allocating scarce resources between prevention and care interventions (World Bank 2000: 3–4). Such cost considerations are explored further in Chapter 7.

We have seen that within development studies there is no consensus on the definition of the term 'scaling up' and the term has been used to denote changes to the organisation itself or to its coverage of the population it is intending to reach. In the case of HIV/AIDS, where appropriate approaches to addressing the epidemic are debated intensely, there are strongly opposing viewpoints as to the best way to approach scaling up. For example, there are tensions between those who argue that a limited number of key interventions should be 'delivered' at a greater scale versus those who contend that addressing HIV/AIDS requires equipping people with the resources and power to reduce their vulnerability. In practice, however, NGOs often derive their policies from both sides of that debate. If scaling up is seen as unfolding over time then an organization's objectives may vary according to different stages of that process, to the level of the epidemic and the overall political and social environment. At each stage, moreover, organizations are confronted with trade-offs and choices, which are the subject of Chapter 3.

CHAPTER THREE

Trade-offs and difficult choices

PRESERVING ORGANIZATIONAL VALUES

The small-scale nature of many NGO activities has in many ways been their strength. A range of NGOs is active in HIV/AIDS, varying from very small organizations to those operating at the national level. Developing typologies of NGOs active in HIV/AIDS is problematic, as many do not fit neatly into specific categories. Nevertheless, one useful typology includes:

- indigenous NGOs established and managed by community 'outsiders'
- indigenous community-based NGOs originated and managed by members of the community (also called community-based organizations or CBOs)
- organizations of people living with HIV/AIDS
- foreign NGOs (Sittitrai 1994).

Perhaps the most effective have been those that have emerged within particular communities. The larger, more professional AIDS organizations certainly have a critical role to play, such as in providing information, influencing government policy and providing support to other organizations. However, their ability to inspire behavioural change is often more limited. As O'Malley and co-authors say of these larger, more professional groups: 'Such groups tend to be technically stronger, have more effective access to decision-makers, and despite higher costs, can often be very cost-efficient because of the scale of their operations . . . but very few such large groups can actually convince a young man to use condoms if he has not tried them before' (O'Malley et al. 1996: 345).

We have seen that there are a number of positive features that represent a comparative advantage for NGOs working on HIV/AIDS, compared to other types of organization, although these characteristics are by no means shared by all NGOs. The commitment of the truly constituency-based organizations to being rooted within their communities, which they often know intimately, enables them to work in a personalized manner with the sensitive and stigmatizing issues raised by HIV/AIDS. NGOs often pay more attention than other actors to ethical considerations raised by HIV/AIDS, such as the need to safeguard confidentiality and to ensure that informed consent is secured. In turn, they are able to come to understand the specific local risk factors for HIV transmission. Without the impediments faced by larger and more visible organizations, such NGOs can work with marginalized groups such as sex workers, drug users and illegal immigrants. Their small size enables them to respond in a flexible way to the rapidly evolving nature of the epidemic, and they can change direction and adapt to lessons learned on the ground. Less weighed down by bureaucracy than their larger or governmental counterparts, they can more easily integrate work across functions, rather than being restricted to single types of activity. NGOs are often more equipped than other types of institution to engage in advocacy regarding HIV/AIDS-related policies, and to combine this role with a more service-oriented one. Finally, their commitment to their communities means that often they provide the only sustained response to the HIV/AIDS epidemic, and are more likely to offer care and support as well as engage in preventive activities.

Therefore the challenge of scaling up activities in HIV/AIDS must address the question of whether such valuable characteristics should and can be preserved as the programme or institution expands. This means not only extending the technical aspects of HIV/AIDS work, but also maintaining the integrity of the processes and values that are the hallmark of NGO approaches to the epidemic.

MAINTAINING QUALITY VERSUS EXPANDING COVERAGE

While there is a danger that increasing coverage may have a knock-on effect in reducing quality, this is not necessarily the case. The FACT/FOCUS Programme in Zimbabwe provides an example of a programme that became stronger as it expanded (see Case Study 11). The expansion reduced the material support and supervision that FACT staff provided, thus increasing a sense of community ownership. In turn, the sustainability and strength of the CBOs increased, as some found additional resources themselves and recruited their own staff.

Expansion may not always bring such opportunities, however, and as NGOs come under increasing pressure to scale up, they may find that increasing coverage puts a strain on maintaining quality. A slight drop in quality may be an inevitable stage of the scaling-up process – that is, in the interest of reaching a greater number of people, some sacrifice of quality is acceptable. This may be particularly the case if many elements or programmes are scaled up simultaneously (International HIV/AIDS Alliance and GlaxoSmithKline 2000b: 10), although ensuring proper planning of the scaling up may limit this risk. The question then becomes whether the quality of a programme drops below an 'acceptable' level and indeed whether such a level can be specified (International HIV/AIDS Alliance and GlaxoSmithKline 2000b: 10). But this will always be difficult to show clearly – as argued above, many NGOs lack sufficient monitoring capacity or data to assess changes in quality as the scaling up proceeds.

One example of an organization that did pay careful attention to monitoring quality during the process of expansion is that of the Asociacion de Salud Integral (ASI) in Guatemala, an organization founded to provide clinical services for those with HIV/AIDS. By enlisting volunteer medical students to collect data, they were able to track changes in quality as a rapid expansion of the counselling and clinical service coverage took place. Analysis of these data indicated that while an increasing number of people were coming to their services for voluntary testing, they were often not returning for their results. Further investigation into the reasons for this revealed that the time between test and results had increased due to the increase in numbers attending. Thus data collected during the process of scaling up on changes in the quality of ASI's work were helpful in guiding a redirection of strategy.

In contrast to the example of ASI, there are documented cases where a rapid increase of coverage has led to a decline in quality. The school-based Anti-AIDS Clubs in Zambia began in the 1980s as a result of a presentation on sex education in high schools by a doctor. Students promoted the idea of setting up such clubs to their friends during the holidays, and the clubs continued to multiply across the nation. Over time, the activities of the Anti-AIDS Clubs in Zambia proliferated rapidly and for a number of reasons they were no longer particularly effective and starting dying out. Realizing the effect of this spontaneous scaling up on quality, the Family Health Trust decided to rethink its scaling-up strategy, and rather than increasing coverage, set about reorganizing support structures and boosting the

Case Study 2   Asociacion de Salud Integral
(Guatemala). Monitoring progress

The Asociacion de Salud Integral (ASI) is a local NGO established in Guatemala City, Guatemala in 1987. Originally known as Asociacion Guatemalteca para la Prevencion y Control de SIDA, the organization was founded by a group of physicians and other healthcare personnel who were concerned about the lack of information on HIV/AIDS available to healthcare workers. Its main mandate is to reduce the impact of HIV/AIDS in Guatemala through education, research and treatment.

A major expansion of ASI's clinical and educational programmes took place after 1995; the organization grew in five years from a staff of six, running one programme in a single public hospital, to a staff of 40 running seven projects, aided by a large group of volunteers. The impetus for the expansion was internal, although the anticipation of a dramatic increase in affected populations was a key reason for the scaling up. Patient numbers had increased by 15 to 20%, waiting time had lengthened and the physical space for counselling and treatment was constrained. It was thus felt imperative to scale up the counselling and treatment programme, including expanding the physical space and serving new target groups (in this case, children and babies). A new weekly clinic accepting 300 children was established. After the scaling-up process was underway the organization experienced a 100% increase in patient load in the year 2000 – reflecting both the increased demand and the greater capacity of ASI services.

ASI's expansion was particularly noteworthy for its attention to ongoing monitoring regarding the impact of the scaling-up exercise. From the beginning, there were concerns about whether the services were responding to the needs of people living with HIV/AIDS. The fact that a group of families of people living with HIV/AIDS is represented on the board of the organization meant that this accountability was structured into their decision-making. Moreover, ASI actively sought alliances with organizations of people living with HIV/AIDS.

Recognizing also that they had collected a great deal of data on their services since the inception of their programmes, but had not fully analysed these, they recruited someone to do so. In addition, a special research programme was established within the clinic, with medical school students recruited to assist professional staff. These volunteers were attracted not only out of commitment to the issue, but also by the greater physical space available. They were especially valuable in collecting data useful for monitoring and evaluation of the scaling up. One of their key findings was that although the demand for voluntary counselling and testing was increasing rapidly, with more and more people wanting to be tested, the service was taking longer to return test results, and therefore the return rate was falling. This clear indicator of diminishing quality was then immediately addressed in the successive scaling up.

This ongoing scaling-up process in the ASI treatment and counselling programme has allowed the organization to gain experience and plan more effectively for the future. ASI's founders conclude that organizations of people living with HIV/AIDS must be involved in any scaling-up programme from the beginning. This generates trust and a sense of empowerment within the community and makes people more willing to participate in education and prevention programmes, and to accept treatment.

quality of an initiative that was already operating at national level. The experience reinforces the view that during a scaling-up process, one may need to concentrate on one dimension – such as quality or coverage – possibly at the expense of the another.

The struggle to maintain quality during the scaling-up process may pose a strain on staff of the organization(s) concerned. As a member of TASO stated: 'It began so well but things got tough when it turned to scaling up'. In some cases, NGOs have realized that a key challenge in scaling up is deciding when to stop. Dr Suniti Solomon of YRG CARE in India has stated, 'One of the most important things for YRG CARE is the quality of services we provide. As a result, we chose to stop expanding our in-patient care when we reached 24 beds so that the quality we provided remains at a high level' (International HIV/ AIDS Alliance and GlaxoSmithKline 2001: 24). Nonetheless, the tendency of NGOs to measure their coverage in relation to their own capacity rather than to overall need is problematic. In a study of scaling up home-based care in Zambia, Nsutebu and colleagues found that one organization had a target of 600 patients, and since in a given year it was able to serve 441 patients, estimated its coverage at 74%. When measured on a population-based method, using the estimated number of AIDS patients and other chronically ill patients requiring home-based care, the coverage estimate was only 7% (Nsutebu et al. 2001).

The dynamic relationship between quality and coverage has been examined within the broader development arena by David Korten,

Case Study 3   Family Health Trust 'Anti-AIDS Clubs'
(Zambia). Boosting quality of an initiative at scale

Students at the David Kaunda Secondary School in Lusaka originated
the idea of creating an Anti-AIDS Club after hearing a talk by a doctor
about HIV/AIDS. They then convinced friends in other schools to adopt
the idea, and the clubs started replicating around the country. The
efforts of the Anti-AIDS Clubs have been assisted by The Family Health
Trust (FHT), a Zambian non-governmental organization (NGO) formed
in 1987 dedicated to preventing the spread of HIV/AIDS while offering
care and support to those already affected. FHT assists the students in
their peer education, which relies on role playing, focus group discussions, games and individual discussions to prevent HIV/AIDS.

The initial approach taken to scaling up the efforts of the Anti-AIDS
Clubs was to encourage the spontaneous replication of the clubs to
broaden their geographic coverage. The decision to scale up was thus
based on the success of the original programme and the evident desire
among young people in Zambia to take positive action about HIV/AIDS.
To strengthen the effectiveness of the peer education efforts, FHT provided training to students who led the Anti-AIDS Clubs and supervised
them through adult facilitators, who are teachers, church leaders or
members of local community groups. Its staff also developed a maga-
zine with basic facts about HIV/AIDS as well as a quarterly newsletter
with articles by young people themselves. To increase the status
attached to the clubs, FHT encouraged the clubs to offer badges and
membership cards. However, the organization soon found that it did not
have the resources to sustain the quality of the initiative as it expanded
rapidly throughout the country. The initiated projects were too numer-
ous and existing staff were constrained, and the clubs themselves
started dying out.

The ultimate approach taken to scaling up by the FHT and the Anti-
AIDS Clubs represents a unique experience among the case studies in
this book. Rather than a focus on expansion or institutional base or programme activity per se, it emphasized increasing the quality of an initiative that had diffused spontaneously from school to school and
encouraging the interest of youth in sustaining the clubs. The first step
in raising quality was to consolidate the field support to the clubs
through a programme of training and supervision based on the development of regional coordination and zonal leaders. FHT provided training of trainers for regional and zonal coordinators and club leaders, who
in turn trained club members. Simultaneously, FHT produced new edu-

cational materials, notably a manual entitled 'Happy, Healthy and Safe', which is easy to use without training for peer education in HIV/AIDS. Finally, recognizing the limited ability of the Anti-AIDS Clubs to reach youth who are out of school (and likely to be more vulnerable to poverty and HIV), another aim of this stage of the scaling up was to intensify outreach to non-members. To achieve the above objectives, the FHT enlisted volunteers who were given a small stipend and a bicycle to help them reach the clubs throughout the zones.

By the year 2000, there were 2561 clubs registered with the Anti-AIDS project, 45% at primary and secondary level, 43% serving out-of-school youth and young adults, and 12% in community schools. Of these, however, only 717 were highly active in the year 2000. The most notable result of the scaling up to date is the increased involvement of young people concerned about, or affected by HIV/AIDS, who are able to initiate their own activities through the support of the FHT. Their efforts illustrate once again the critical links between care, support and prevention in HIV/AIDS, and provide an unusual example of how pro-grammes initially aimed at prevention can expand into care and support. For example, some Anti-AIDS Clubs have moved into income generat-ing, creating fish farms and groceries, and using the revenue to help orphans and young people affected by HIV/AIDS with school fees. Other clubs reached out to their friends out of school by initiating literacy classes. Perhaps most importantly, the increased scale of such activity by young people themselves contributes to raising awareness of HIV/AIDS in the wider communities in which they live. In the words of Dixter Kaluba, this has helped to familiarize youth with problems asso-ciated with epidemic and thus 'young people don't feel the epidemic is so distant' (Dixter Kaluba, FHT, Horizons/Alliance Seminar).

One major challenge the initiative has faced is a persistent gender imbalance in the membership of the clubs, with boys more involved than girls, reflecting the increased reluctance of girls to broach the sen-sitive topic of HIV/AIDS. Reaching out-of-school youth has also proved difficult, particularly in the absence of material incentives.

Because the Anti-AIDS Clubs represented an experiment, there was little upon which to base an initial evaluation. In some respects, evalua-tions of the Anti-AIDS Club initiative since their inception have been dis-appointing, in that they have revealed that sexual behaviour among young people has not changed as a result of membership in the clubs and condom use has not increased. At the same time, the experience of the FHT points to the need to take a broad and multifaceted approach to evaluation. For example, by looking at reporting to health services for

> sexually transmitted infections (STIs), evaluators found that more young people reported to health centres for screening and treatment of STIs.
>
> In conclusion, the scaling-up experience of the Anti-AIDS Clubs provides an example of a professional NGO supporting and motivating the spread of a spontaneous initiative among people concerned about the epidemic's impact on their country. Having replicated and expanded naturally, the Anti-AIDS Clubs profited by the involvement of the NGO not only in terms of material support, but to maintain the quality of their peer education and to sustain the early enthusiasm of founders of the Anti-AIDS Clubs.

who attempted to draw out the shared characteristics among five community-based projects in Asia, which successfully expanded the scale of their operations.[16] Korten concludes that there is no single blueprint for scaling up, but organizations go through a number of common stages during expansion (as illustrated in Figure 5), each of which entails a learning process. The first is 'learning to be effective', when the organization learns what strategies are effective among particular populations. At this stage errors are made, but effectiveness increases steadily; efficiency has not yet been achieved and coverage is likely to be relatively low. At the next stage, the organization is 'learning to be efficient', and unit costs tend to fall. Only in the third and final stage does the organization move into expansion, and there is likely to be some loss of effectiveness and efficiency as the expansion occurs. As the organizational growth continues, it is likely that average costs will tend to rise, raising the issue of when it is optimal to continue to expand rather than replicating the project at a smaller scale. The extent to which this 'trial and error' process is permitted and learning is encouraged depends on both the external environment – in terms of finance and political commitment – and the internal characteristics of the organization, which is addressed in Part III.

A QUESTION OF FOCUS

One key decision NGOs need to make as they scale up their programmes is what social groups and interventions they need to focus on. Focus requires trade-offs, in that no organization can concentrate on all aspects of the epidemic at the same time. Moreover,

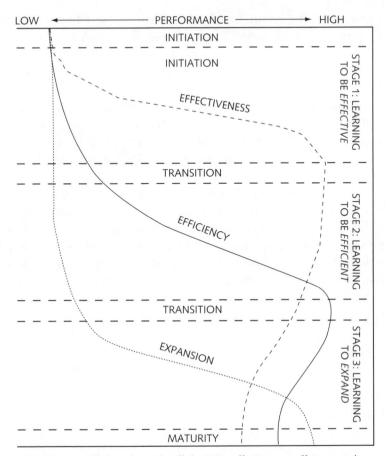

Note: There are likely to be trade-offs between effectiveness, efficiency and expansion which will lead to some loss of effectiveness as efficiency increases, and to losses in both effectiveness and efficiency during expansion

Figure 5 Programme learning curves
Source: Korten (1980).

appropriate areas for focus are likely to change over time and with the evolution of the epidemic. Many ethical questions come into play in determining, in particular, who should benefit from the scaling-up process. In an advanced epidemic, for example, where everyone is affected, if an NGO focuses on care and support, should they focus on delivering high-quality interventions to a few, or should everyone be offered a minimal service? The answers to these questions may depend on the accountability of the organization and whether it is a small, local NGO or a national one. Answers to these and other questions NGOs need to ask before scaling up are also dependent on the cultural and political context in which NGOs are operating, which will be discussed further in Chapter 6.

In a young epidemic, infections are likely to be associated with specific behaviour patterns. What is the appropriate focus of prevention activities in this context – increasing the scale by intensifying work with a limited number of people who exhibit these behaviours, or broadening the focus so a wider population is aware that HIV is spreading? The first may have the associated risk of identifying and perhaps stigmatizing the affected group. The latter may not have a significant effect on epidemic dynamics.

If scaling up is envisioned as a process, then NGOs need to consider the choices and trade-offs to be made along the way. It may be necessary for NGOs to sacrifice some quality to the goal of increasing the coverage of their programmes. But this risk is reduced if NGOs develop effective monitoring systems to detect such dips in quality, in the way that ASI in Guatemala has done, for example (Case Study 2). The nature of the choices to be made will depend to a large extent on the choice of strategy for scaling up, which is the topic of Chapter 4.

PART II

STRATEGIC CONSIDERATIONS

CHAPTER FOUR

Strategies for scaling up of relevance to HIV/AIDS

APPROACHES TO SCALING UP IN THE DEVELOPMENT LITERATURE: RELEVANCE TO HIV/AIDS

In describing the mechanisms or pathways through which develop-ment NGOs in general can have broader impact, Robert Chambers, an advocate of applying participatory approaches to development, is quoted as stating that:

> An NGO can achieve wider impacts in many ways including expanding its operations; introducing or developing technologies which spread; developing and using approaches which are then adopted by other NGOs and/or by government; influencing changes in government and donor policies and actions; and gaining and disseminating understanding about development.

> (Drabek 1987)

In looking at the HIV/AIDS epidemic specifically, it is evident that NGOs have exerted influence on the general approaches to HIV/AIDS by means of each of the above pathways. The emphasis on and need for home care, for example, was initiated by NGOs, as was the emphasis on the ethical need to combine counselling with voluntary testing, and indeed the whole notion of 'safe sex' and its promotion (O'Malley et al. 1996). Similarly, it is largely due to suc-cessful NGO advocacy that an increasing number of donors now rec-ognize the need to support and finance AIDS care and treatment, as well as prevention, which they were previously reluctant to do. Thanks to the efforts of NGOs, policy makers have a greater under-standing of the social determinants of the epidemic and its effects on communities and individuals. Global alliances of NGOs active in HIV/AIDS have recorded significant progress in pushing for conces-sions in the prices of drugs manufactured by multinational pharma-ceutical companies. Yet, as stated above, much of this impact has been spontaneous, rather than a reflection of deliberate strategy to scale up the impact of NGOs.

Within the context of development thinking generally, a number of authors have addressed the question of deliberate strategies to increase the scale and widen the impact of NGO activities. John Clark, for example, formerly of OXFAM but now working at the World Bank on NGOs, argues that there are essentially three pathways available to NGOs: project replication; building grassroots movements; and influencing policy (Clark 1991, 1992).

Howes and Sattar (1992) make the useful distinction between organizational or programme growth as opposed to achieving impact by means of transferring programmes to or supporting other organizations. Myers (1992), in an analysis of scaling up early childhood development programmes, develops a terminology characterizing the pace and nature of expansion. He uses the term 'planned expansion' to refer to the process of implementing a particular model in a number of geographic areas once it has been pilot tested; 'explosion' to denote the sudden initiation of a large-scale programme or intervention without any policy or organization preparation beforehand; and 'association' to mean expanding a programme size through common efforts and alliances among a group of organizations, each of whom develop similar programmes but tailor them to the needs of specific communities or populations.

Other authors have pointed out that it is not the content of services alone that can be replicated or expanded, but underlying approaches or ideas, and this is particularly relevant to work on HIV/AIDS. Chambers (1992), for example, refers to what he calls 'self-spreading and self-improving strategies', whereby good practice (such as participatory approaches) is gradually extended through other organizations, in effect transforming their approach.[17] Wazir and van Oudenhoven (1998) use the term 'concept replication' to denote a similar process.

In the early 1990s, Edwards and Hulme, struck by the lack of analyses of NGO efforts to scale up in developing countries, convened a number of workshops under the auspices of the University of Manchester and the Save the Children Fund. These brought together a diverse range of case studies of scaling up by both Northern and Southern NGOs, and include the presentation of a number of think pieces on scaling-up strategies more generally.[18] In their efforts to synthesize the findings from these studies, Edwards and Hulme developed a threefold conceptual framework of strategies NGOs have used to scale up, namely: *additive* strategies, which imply an increase in the size of a programme or organization; *multiplicative* strategies, which do not necessarily imply growth but achieve impact through influence, networking, policy and legal reform or training; and *diffusive* approaches, where spread tends to be informal and spontaneous.

The question arises as to how these understandings of NGO efforts to scale up in development broadly can be applied to the field of HIV/AIDS. There are particular complications in that few areas of development are associated with such stigma, making it difficult to address the sensitive behavioural determinants of the disease and the social prejudices which make provision of care and support for those affected so challenging. Moreover, within HIV/AIDS there are opposing tendencies, as described in Chapter 2, between those who subscribe to a medical model of health (and thus focus on delivery of large-scale interventions) and those who put more emphasis on a social model of health (and focus on addressing the social and behavioural determinants of ill health).

A PROPOSED FRAMEWORK FOR SCALING UP IN HIV/AIDS

To the author's knowledge, there has been no systematic analysis of approaches or philosophies to scaling up specific to the HIV/AIDS sector. In an effort to distil the findings from more general analyses of scaling up development NGOs to processes relevant to HIV/AIDS, the following framework is proposed (summarized in Figure 6). Five different types of strategy are envisioned, represented on a continuum along which the original organization that initiates the scaling-up effort becomes less and less involved. The continuum also presents a gradation of strategies that become increasingly abstract in nature, making it difficult to measure their impact.

This typology is of ideal types and does not represent the evolution of specific organizations. Indeed, any given NGO may employ several of these strategies simultaneously, and to different types of HIV/AIDS programmes as is appropriate to particular time periods, geographic areas or social groups.

STRATEGY 1: ORGANIZATIONAL EXPANSION

This category refers to the simplest form of scaling-up activity. It reflects the effort of one organization acting on its own, rather than

	Strategy 1: Organizational expansion	Strategy 2: Catalysing role a) technically b) financially	Strategy 3: Diffusion	Strategy 4: Influencing policy	Strategy 5: Mainstreaming in development
Main objectives	Diversify ▪ geographical area ▪ social groups ▪ functions	Expand range of services provided	Spread: ▪ concept ▪ approach ▪ technology	Influencing policy climate	Legitimize discussion of HIV/AIDS and sexuality broadly
Type of organization involved	Initial organizational only	▪ Government (service) ▪ Private sector ▪ Other NGO ▪ CBOs	Any	▪ Government ▪ Donors ▪ NGOs	All development institutions

Figure 6   A proposed typology of scaling up in HIV/AIDS

attempts to work with other institutions. Organizational expansion entails increasing scale either by reaching a greater number of people, social groups or geographic areas, or expanding the functions or activity of the organization. This may include, for example, developing a pilot project that is then expanded to a greater geographic area, or the opening of branches of the same organization in different locations. Such a strategy for scaling up usually relies on an expanded funding base or increased voluntary contributions from constituents.

In the general field of development, perhaps the most famous example of this first strategy is the Bangladesh Rural Advancement Committee (BRAC), which began in 1972 and is now one of the largest Southern NGOs with a staff of over 12 000 and a budget of close to $23 million, reaching millions of people throughout Bangladesh. BRAC has achieved this scale through careful expansion of both the types of activity it undertakes (diversifying from economic activity into child survival and women's health for example) and by moving into different geographic regions of Bangladesh. According to one analysis of this scaling-up process, quality was not sacrificed (Howes and Sattar 1992), perhaps owing to BRAC's careful approach based on experimenting through pilot projects, learning from them and then replicating successful practices on a greater scale (Uvin 1995).

Within the more specific setting of HIV/AIDS organizations, extending to other population groups has been an explicit orientation of the scaling-up objectives of a number of NGOs. For example, Colectivo Sol, an NGO based in Mexico City, started by focusing its efforts on self-identified gay men, but went on to initiate educational programmes and other services for a wider group, including young people and other NGOs. Similarly, staff at the ASI in Guatemala felt the need to extend their clinical services to children and babies. Their expansion of the programme was driven by increased demand for their services, projections of an impending acceleration in the incidence of HIV/AIDS, and their perception that they either had to admit failure and close, or expand to cope with their rising caseload. Similarly, the Anti-AIDS Clubs supported by the NGO Family Health Trust in Zambia started in schools but successfully extended to out-of-school youth through its scaling-up process, although it is much more costly and difficult to gain access to these young people than those in school.

STRATEGY 2: CATALYSING OTHERS

This strategy refers to deliberate efforts on the part of one organization to work with other organizations, either within the same sector or different sectors, in order to influence the nature or scope of their service provision. This could entail developing relationships with government (particularly in terms of the latter's service provision, not policy), the private sector or, perhaps most usually, with other NGOs. One of the most common occurrences in this context is for an organization to develop a model which the government is then persuaded to adopt.

This category would encompass the work of NGO support organizations, which see their main contribution as offering technical, financial and social support to smaller organizations. An NGO may persuade another NGO to integrate an HIV/AIDS programme into its health or developmental activities.[19] The strategy may also entail providing expertise or guidance based on greater experience in HIV/AIDS, or may be more related to organizational development. An explicit part of KANCO's mandate in Kenya, for example, is to assist member organizations in strategic planning, organizational development and financial accounting.

In some cases, organizations may begin as direct service providers but subsequently move into supporting other organizations financially.[20] For example, PSG (Zimbabwe), in the course of its scaling up, has developed a system of national and regional grants. The organization supports about 130 projects, of which an estimated 60% are in prevention and 40% in mitigating the effects of the epidemic, although the latter is growing rapidly. In addition, PSG provides training in grant management, including establishing effective management systems, guidance on project application, the design of review forms and better financial and progress reporting.

Unequal power relations between the more professionally-oriented NGOs offering assistance in capacity-building and programme design and the organizations receiving the support can hamper such efforts. In most cases, the former have definite advantages in terms of access to finance and information that may translate into differential input in setting the agenda for the programme. Where careful attention is paid to redressing, or at least recognizing, imbalances between organizations in terms of access to information, resources or power, and where credit for success is fairly given, the results of such a catalytic strategy can be extremely positive.

In the first stage of the scaling up of the South India AIDS Action Project (SIAAP), when 'NGOs were afraid of entering HIV/AIDS', SIAAP adopted a 'catalyst' strategy, concentrating its activities from 1991 on encouraging development NGOs to enter the field of HIV. It did so by offering support in terms of the technical issues of HIV, as well as institutional capacity-building and limited funding. By the end of this period, in 1996, it had worked with 42 NGOs in Tamil Nadu, Karnataka and Andhra Pradesh to integrate HIV into their work. Later, it found that the provision of funds put SIAAP in an uncomfortable donor role, and it subsequently moved away from this function and restricted its support to technical issues.

The experience of KIMIRINA in Ecuador was almost opposite to that of SIAAP in that when they only provided technical support to other organisations the latter's commitment to HIV/AIDS was relatively weak and KIMIRINA therefore subsequently moved into offering financial support as well. Staff of KIMIRINA found that even large organizations with significant budgets can be influenced by the contribution of budgets earmarked for HIV/AIDS, however modest. In their view, only once an organization has a high level of awareness and strong commitment will technical support suffice in motivating activity on HIV/AIDS (see Case Study 4).

The International HIV/AIDS Alliance (Case Study 11) employs this strategy at an international level. It sees its broad mandate as scaling up community response to HIV/AIDS internationally. To this end the Alliance works through 'linking organizations' that it supports both financially and technically. These organizations in turn reach out and support local NGOs in their settings technically,

Case Study 4   KIMIRINA (Ecuador). Catalysing a community-based response to HIV/AIDS in Ecuador

Although the incidence of HIV has been increasing rapidly in recent years in Ecuador, HIV/AIDS prevalence is still relatively low and there are relatively few NGOs specializing in HIV/AIDS. Thus the strategy for scaling up described here is one of a 'catalyst' role, specifically aiming to build the capacity in development-related NGOs working in a range of sectors to address HIV.

In 1995, an Ecuadorian development NGO called COMUNIDEC, founded ten years earlier to create solidarity between the various ethnic and disadvantaged social groups and encourage communities to respond to social problems in Ecuador, established the Programme for AIDS Initiative (UNAIDS 2001). With the assistance of the International HIV/AIDS Alliance, COMUNIDEC's programme aimed to support HIV prevention and care programmes throughout Ecuador. The Alliance sponsored a series of workshops that aimed to improve HIV-related NGOs' relationships with business, media, government, local health services and other NGOs. COMUNIDEC remained a linking organization of the Alliance until 2000, when it ceased its AIDS programming to return to its original mandate. A new organization, called KIMIRINA (a Quichua word that means 'coming together to do something'), became the new linking organization of the Alliance.

Corporacion KIMIRINA is a national NGO with a mandate to encourage the participation of local actors to respond to sexual health problems, including HIV/AIDS. In 1998, it realized that the best way to achieve this would be to establish partnerships with other development-, rights- or gender-related organizations. KIMIRINA approached NGOs with a large network of services with the aim of helping them to incorporate AIDS into the services they already promoted. Thus it began to provide a support system, including training, technical support, institutional stengthening and practical resources to organizations that work in HIV/AIDS or that are interested in that field. Most of the assistance KIMIRINA provides is in the form of training and technical assistance, including information about sexuality, sexually transmitted diseases and HIV/AIDS, and skills such as counselling training, project planning and evaluation, and how to do participatory community assessments. Notably, KIMIRINA also provides key support to help organizations strengthen their institutional capacity in areas such as accountancy, administration and project management. The assistance that KIMIRINA provides at all of these levels helps to build the capacity of the local

NGOs and CBOs and promotes the ability of the local organizations to negotiate strategic relations with other local, national and regional actors.

KIMIRINA also began to provide financial support, and found that this increased its influence in encouraging even large organizations with significant budgets to address HIV/AIDS. Assistance is of two kinds, either open or closed (UNAIDS 2001). An open request for proposals (RFP) is intended to encourage organizations that do not have experience in HIV/AIDS to solicit support. A closed RFP is designed to support organizations which previously had grants and thus to support their ongoing work. In both cases, KIMIRINA has developed strict criteria for support (UNAIDS 2001), in that organizations requesting finance must be able to: generate knowledge useful to other organisations; provide prevention or care where there is unmet demand; and become a technical reference centre in their region.

In addition, they need to show interest in working in HIV/AIDS, have a transparent organizational structure, be open to sharing their experiences with other NGOs and be a non-profit organization.

The broad coverage of the organizations which KIMIRINA supports ensures that it reaches sectors of the population it would not be able to reach alone. These include peasant and indigenous women, young people outside the formal education system and vulnerable groups such as transvestites, prisoners, truck drivers, sex workers, men who have sex with men and migrants (UNAIDS 2001). KIMIRINA also actively seeks cooperation with organizations that have strong links to local and national governments and therefore have the potential for influencing policy making (UNAIDS 2001).

Over the seven years since the inception of the initiative begun by COMUNIDEC and later continued by the independent NGO KIMIRINA, the programme has supported 110 projects within 41 organizations in 14 provinces. As UNAIDS summarizes the impact of this work:

> *NGOs and CBOs already working with women and local develop-*
> *ment (but with no experience in AIDS) have been able to assess*
> *the AIDS-related needs of their communities, and begin, or take*
> *over existing AIDS work. In particular, these organisations have*
> *been able to move beyond AIDS awareness-raising campaigns to*
> *programmes addressing: (1) individual and social vulnerability; and*
> *(2) behavioural change.*
>
> *(UNAIDS 2001: 44)*

organizationally and through exchange of information within and between countries.

A number of organizations provide technical support to other organizations by arranging for exchange visits, both within a country or internationally. This approach is critical to the PSG's training to community volunteers in Southern Africa, for example. It is also an integral part of the Salvation Army's 'concept transfer' approach (described in Case Study 6).

HIV/AIDS prevention efforts may be most effective if integrated into existing infrastructures that already operate at a large scale across a range of sectors. Thus NGOs may seek to 'catalyse' those existing services to address HIV/AIDS. Indeed, seeking ways of combining HIV/AIDS interventions with delivery in other sectors, as opposed to focusing on scaling up individual HIV/AIDS interventions independently, may yield 'economies of scope' whereby lower costs and greater efficiency are achieved than through separate delivery (Kumaranayake 2000).

Yet, as argued by Watts and Kumaranayake (1999) in an article in the *Lancet*, the potential for integrating HIV/AIDS programmes into other services, whether in education, reproductive health, family planning or sex education, is often not fully exploited. They argue that in the short term, effective activities that can be scaled up quickly need to be identified, including using private sector (workplaces, unions) and informal networks involving religious and community groups. Taking advantage of such opportunities could help to increase the access of different social and geographical groups to specific activities (Watts and Kumaranayake 1999).

STRATEGY 3: DIFFUSION

The third type of strategy represents an effort to broaden impact by encouraging other organizations to adopt a particular concept, approach or technology. Diffusion is explicitly more abstract than previous strategies because it does not entail expanding one's own or influencing others' specific programmes or activities. Rather, it consists of spreading ideas or methodologies. Included among this wide set of strategies would be spreading the concept of peer education, community counselling or the promotion of male and female condoms (as technologies). This can entail either planned or spontaneous effort, but by and large the initiating organization is less directly involved in the implementation of the programme and works instead through influencing others. Outside the field of HIV/AIDS, this strategy has been very effective in promoting, for example, community-based rehabilitation approaches or reproductive health (particularly in influencing family planning organizations that previously provided highly top-down, vertical programmes). At issue is not always increasing budgets or introducing new technologies, but influencing the attitudes of providers and sensitizing them to the new approach.

As the following example of SIAAP illustrates, the notion of community counselling in HIV/AIDS was foreign to India before SIAAP initiated a diffusion strategy to spread and legitimize the concept. Existing government sexually transmitted disease facilities were not attracting patients – particularly women – due to the lack of a receptive atmosphere. SIAAP saw an opportunity to introduce counselling to break communication barriers between doctors and patients. Lacking expertise on approaches to community counselling in India, SIAAP staff initially sought technical input from a number of international institutions. In this case, government saw clearly the advantage of potentially increasing demand for their services. An arrangement was agreed whereby the government pays the salaries of counsellors who are trained and supervised by SIAAP. As a result of their efforts SIAAP has received requests from governments in neighbouring states for similar assistance. SIAAP's staff conclude that: 'SIAAP's counselling programme has been acknowledged and appreciated by the established medical system and endorsed by the Indian government' (Case Study 5).

At the international level, the Salvation Army's HIV/AIDS programme seeks to help communities to cope with the epidemic, and to this end facilitates exchange visits across regions and countries to share experience. In the course of this process, 'facilitation teams' explore key concepts related to the epidemic with local stakeholders. In so doing, the organization has endeavoured to foster greater willingness and capacity among communities to address HIV/AIDS (Case Study 6).

In Zambia, the Family Health Trust (Case Study 4) has also used this strategy to diffuse the model of the Anti-AIDS Clubs to other schools in other locations. And ASI, which was the only clinical service in Guatemala providing integrated services to people living with HIV/AIDS, made an explicit part of their strategy for scaling up to influence other clinical services to incorporate a similar approach (Case Study 2).

Case Study 5 South India AIDS Action Programme.
Diffusing the concept of community counselling

The South India AIDS Action Programme (SIAAP) represents an interesting case of an NGO which made its first impact in HIV/AIDS by taking a confrontational approach to government authorities, but subsequently ended up working closely with government through convincing them to integrate counselling into the HIV/AIDS clinical services. This 'diffusion' of the concept of community counselling was highly influential, and ultimately spread to three states of Southern India.

SIAAP emerged in 1988 out of a confrontation with local authorities when 30 HIV-positive female sex workers in the city of Chennai, South India, were imprisoned. By the time their case was taken to trial by the journalist who broke the story, nearly 900 HIV-positive women were incarcerated in the state of Tamil Nadu. In July 1990, the court ordered all the women to be released and recommended that no person should be detained on the basis of HIV infection. At this time there were no HIV-related education, prevention or support services available. A link with a community health initiative as well as with official social support services was established in 1991 to bring existing NGOs together and help them develop strategies to address the epidemic. This led to the founding of SIAAP as an independent NGO.

Although the SIAAP initiative had started with advocacy, it was clear that HIV interventions had to include education on safer sex practices, including condom use and improved treatment access for sexually transmitted infections (STIs), and to reduce prejudice and stigma surrounding HIV. SIAAP moved on from a confrontational strategy at the beginning of the epidemic to a 'catalyst' approach in trying to convince development-related NGOs to integrate HIV into their work. Having largely succeeded in its attempts to get NGOs and governments to address HIV issues, the SIAAP management began to consider the future direction of the organization. SIAAP staff recognized the pressing need to develop community-based counselling strategies that were different from providing information and advice and included a strong orientation towards human rights and personal growth. This led to SIAAP's creation of the first structured, continuing and long-term training programme. With this experience, it became clear that structured long-term training and supervision was a critical component of sustainable interventions in HIV. It was equally apparent that one-off training sessions were hopelessly inadequate, especially in process-oriented areas.

In 1996, recognizing that expertise within India on counselling was limited, SIAAP initiated a close collaboration with government health services. Government hospitals had STI departments but people were not using the services because of the stigma attached, the lack of a receptive atmosphere and non-existent counselling services, and women were not attending at all. Moreover, government STI doctors felt unappreciated given these facilities' under-utilization. An arrangement was then reached whereby SIAAP provided all training and supervision of new counsellors, but the government absorbed the full costs of their employment.

An alliance with an international training institution, the Gestalt Foundation in the Netherlands, helped consolidate this counselling programme. A consultant from that institution visited SIAAP the following year and recommended that SIAAP expand its counselling services and offered training and supervisory support to the initiative in the first two years.

As SIAAP expanded its counselling efforts, it learned that counsellors from affected communities were the most effective counsellors, even if they had less education or experience. They also found that community and hospital counsellors encouraged people to use services, thus raising demand for these services.

Through these extensive partnerships with government and the Gestalt Foundation, SIAAP was successful in diffusing the notion of HIV/AIDS counselling, which until then had been an unknown concept in India. Counselling came to be recognized as a critical bridge between preventing HIV transmission and caring for those with HIV/AIDS. Neighbouring states, upon seeing the success of the programme, became interested in initiating similar programmes in their states. By the end of this period, 82 counsellors were providing services in government hospitals across the three states of South India.

Case Study 6   The Salvation Army.
'Concept transfer' approach

The Salvation Army, an international faith-based organization active in social welfare, provides regionally based support to local field programmes in the area of HIV/AIDS, health and development. The goal of the HIV/AIDS work has been to support and expand local community capacity development for care and prevention, while at the same time influencing policy. The main strategy used is participatory programme design with local communities to help them to respond to HIV/AIDS. A critical complementary approach is using exchange visits that focus on building local strengths, and transferring these lessons learned and ideas generated to other communities. Its scaling-up approach thus exemplifies the strategy of 'diffusion' described in this chapter. The organization has now established 88 programmes in HIV/AIDS in 37 different countries, reaching an estimated 4 million people.

The Salvation Army's work emerged from an integrated home-based care and community prevention initiative in Zambia developed at Chikankata Hospital from 1987 to 1990, when HIV was starting to take hold. Over the next three years, a local response to the epidemic was nurtured and grew into a home-care programme. By 1990, communities were implementing change strategies and measuring their own change. This experience formed the basis of a wider initiative of 12 countries in Africa by the Salvation Army's International Headquarters Health Services to develop what they call a 'concept transfer' process to expand the response to HIV/AIDS. As they describe it, 'concept transfer' denotes building local capacity and culture, rather than actually replicating specific activities. That is: 'The organization cannot "do" the work – people-centred approaches provoke growth of a local movement that diffuses, sometimes explosively, across community and organizational boundaries.'

The philosophy behind the Salvation Army's current work in HIV/AIDS is that communities contain some of their own answers to the challenges posed by HIV, but these have to be elicited. Thus their approach is highly participatory, engaging community members who may be concerned about, but have no knowledge of, HIV to stimulate a wider public discussion of the disease and its social consequences, and most importantly, what people can do to address it. The programme thus 'facilitates a response' rather than intervening directly. Once a response is established in one location, community members from that initiative are supported by the Salvation Army to travel to other locations within the same country or internationally to share their experience. Thus a main outcome of this approach is the creation of a regional resource pool of people from within field programmes with capacity to implement programmes as well as to facilitate programme development in other areas.

The success of the approach is monitored through on-site visits and participatory evaluations. However, few data are available regarding the impact on HIV/AIDS directly, except in some locations such as Chikankata Hospital in Zambia where sero-prevalence rates with people in specific risk situations have been continuously monitored for more than a decade. Qualitative indicators chosen by local communities are also used, and these show capacity for local response, such as action for care and community capacity to cope. The Salvation Army regards the fact that it has received many requests for assistance from communities, health and development organizations as an indicator of progress.

STRATEGY 4: INFLUENCING POLICY AND LEGISLATION

On a yet larger scale, organizations may seek to deliberately engage with the policies or legislative activities of governments or of influential donor organizations. They may do so via efforts to shape the public debate on a particular issue, such as through outreach to the media so as to increase the understanding of the social determinants of HIV/AIDS or its impact, or in order to reduce stigma associated with the disease. Alternatively, actors may seek to gain influence via coalition building and knowledge exchange to increase the collective demands of civil society on the state within the arena of HIV/AIDS. For example, KANCO – a national network of NGOs, CBOs and religious organizations concerned about HIV/AIDS in Kenya – aims both to complement government responses as well as to push for a more conducive policy environment. It provides capacity-building to member organizations and operates as a clearing house to provide accurate and up-to-date information on HIV/AIDS. Similarly, ASI and members of a coordinating body of 28 organizations in Guatemala have been lobbying for a more humane HIV/AIDS law, and their efforts bore fruit with the passing of that law in February 2000. And in the Philippines, PHANSuP has lobbied for the full implementation of the existing HIV/AIDS law and held workshops in partnership with government on its application.

Among the strategies discussed so far, this is the most explicitly political. Moreover, trying to influence policy or legislation may at times require a confrontational approach. For example, the organization SIAAP began through efforts to obtain the release of HIV-positive women illegally imprisoned in South India, and it did so through legal challenges in the courts, as well as raising awareness among the public at large. Similarly, the fact that the social security system in Guatemala now offers care and treatment was achieved through lawsuits. A number of initiatives of scaling up harm reduction have also relied on legal strategies and efforts to keep the police at bay. Harm-reduction policies are also particularly relevant where HIV is mainly spread through injecting drug use. There is evidence that needle exchange schemes have a significant impact on reducing HIV transmission, but in many countries where this is the primary route of transmission, drug use is illegal and therefore needle exchange is particularly difficult to implement.

Some organizations may not initially engage in advocacy activities when they start work, but advocacy may become an explicit part of the scaling-up process over time as they encounter obstacles or particular opportunities or needs. For example, the International HIV/AIDS Alliance based in the UK began to find ways to influence donor policies through taking part in formal consultation processes on international instruments such as the Programme of Action adopted at the International Conference on Population and Development in Cairo in 1994. The Programme of Action focused on reproductive health and human rights, and initially did not take into account the broader issues of care and vulnerability relating to HIV. By taking an active part in the international monitoring and consultation processes following the adoption of the Programme of Action, the Alliance, which was the only HIV-specific organization included in the consultations, was able to influence discussions so that the specific issues of HIV/AIDS were not overlooked.

One of the Alliance's linking organizations, KIMIRINA in Ecuador (Case Study 4), after several years of existence focusing primarily on catalysing small CBOs, began to initiate some advocacy activities as it increased its scale of operations and established a more solid institutional base.

NGOs have also used this strategy when working to exert influence on governments and pharmaceutical companies concerning policies relating to access to medication for those with HIV/AIDS. Most have proceeded by forging national, regional and international coalitions comprising developing country governments and activists combined with international NGOs and consumer groups to lobby for price concessions and greater access to treatment. As noted in Chapter 1, these efforts bore fruit with the decision at the 2001 World Trade Organization meetings in Doha, Qatar, to allow compulsory licensing (which would allow local pharmaceutical manufacturers to produce generic versions of patented antiretroviral drugs for the domestic market) in the context of public health emergencies. Because of such advocacy efforts, multinational pharmaceutical corporations have increasingly been offering price concessions on HIV/AIDS-related pharmaceuticals to developing countries.

STRATEGY 5: MAINSTREAMING IN DEVELOPMENT

Related to, yet going beyond, the fourth set of strategies is the effort to permeate all development sectors with concern for and attention to HIV/AIDS and its implications. The explicit objective of such strategies is to widen the narrowly sectoral approach to HIV/AIDS by engaging the decision-making bodies and organizations across relevant sectors as well as seeking channels of implementation beyond the health sector. More of a development focus to AIDS efforts may also encourage a greater public understanding of the social context that puts individuals at risk of HIV/AIDS, discussed in preceding chapters, including poverty, lack of education and ill health. This would also encompass less tangible and more hidden problems such as inequitable gender relations, including women's economic dependence on men, poor self-esteem or lack of control over how and when sex (and conception) takes place. For although one needs to change social norms more broadly in order to slow the spread of the disease, it is often the poorest communities or those individuals with the least decision-making power in society who are most affected by it.[21]

It may also be necessary to work with mainstream institutions involved in administration of the law and justice to address the rights issues that HIV/AIDS raises. Widespread employment-related discrimination in countries with little legal protection has been countered by a number of NGOs working in HIV/AIDS. Working with the police on how they respond to and deal with victims of domestic violence is also critically important. Organizations such as TASO in Uganda (see Case Study 8), which sees its main mandate as helping communities deal with HIV/AIDS, found over the course of its scaling up that it needed to deal with legal rights of both those with HIV and widows who, because of their lack of right to inherit property, were left impoverished after the deaths of their husbands.

NGOs focusing on AIDS often find themselves ill equipped to deal with this broader development context of the pandemic.[22] Conversely, development NGOs often do not take on HIV/AIDS efforts because they see it as a health problem outside their own area of expertise, a problem affecting particular individuals only rather than communities as a whole, or they may lack the financial and technical resources to do so (Sittitrai 1994). This is not to say that HIV/AIDS-specific NGOs should be advised to take on development activities previously not in their mandate. A more effective strategy is likely to involve NGOs working in other areas to address HIV/AIDS so that, in the words of Kevin Orr of the Alliance 'they don't make the same mistakes we did'.

The International HIV/AIDS Alliance has implicitly adopted this strategy in the majority of countries in which it works by choosing broad development organizations, rather than AIDS-specific organizations as linking organizations. Out of the 220 organizations the Alliance had supported by 1996, for example, 200 were general health or development organizations (Case Study 11). Although the Alliance found this strategy more effective, it notes that the associated costs of working with organizations not specialized in HIV/AIDS is often higher, initially at least. In its experience, however, this strategy is appropriate for both low prevalence countries, which may see HIV/AIDS as an issue that may emerge in the medium to long term, as well as higher prevalence countries. In both settings, a wide range of other concerns may consume more attention, from helping young people to get jobs, to gender violence to achieving clear water supplies. Thus linking HIV/AIDS with contextual and development issues, such as gender relations and poverty, has been a key strategy of the Alliance in both types of settings. AMSED in Morocco, for example, a development NGO and linking organization of the Alliance, is collaborating with income generating organizations because they are already mobilized and Morocco lacks organizations working in communities across the country that have expertise in HIV/AIDS.

Finally, PACT (in collaboration with the Alliance) illustrates another example of this strategy – also from an international level – as it specifically helps NGOs involved neither in health nor HIV/AIDS to address AIDS (Case Study 7).

Such a strategy is not without its critics, however. Ainsworth and Teokul (2000) argue, for example, that in poor developing countries with high prevalence of HIV/AIDS, where resource constraints are most evident and state capacity weak, encouraging non-health ministries to address HIV/AIDS may be spreading resources too thinly and may not be cost-effective. 'AIDS mortality may strike every sector of the economy; but this does not necessarily imply that adding AIDS prevention and mitigation to every ministry's programme will be a cost-effective way of reducing the epidemic,' They argue instead that a selective number of interventions should be scaled up to national level by governments and pursued vigorously for achievable outcomes. Their argument emphasizes governmental strategies and is not specifically applied to NGOs, which may be better able to take on additional work in HIV/AIDS, given their flexibility and relatively small size compared to governments. Moreover, Ainsworth and Teokul do stress the importance of integrating HIV/AIDS into poverty reduction strategies, which is now becoming more widespread.

It should be noted that any one organization may engage in a number of the above strategies simultaneously, and there may be overlap between the various categories. Moreover, the staging of the continuum is not intended to imply a chronological progression, as individual organizations may, after assessing their own comparative advantage and environment, decide that any one of these broad categories of scaling up may be the most appropriate place to start.

The following example of the AIDS Support Organisation in Uganda illustrates that approaches to scaling up may evolve over time, reflecting the level of the epidemic, the NGO's perception of need in the society in which they are working, and the lessons they learn from their own and others' experience.

Case Study 7 Private Agencies Cooperating
Together (PACT). PACT's AIDS Corps: integrating
HIV/AIDS work into development

The main objective of the newly established programme of the organization entitled Private Agencies Cooperating Together (PACT) is to keep international attention focused on the HIV/AIDS epidemic and to mobilize resources to fight it. It achieves this goal primarily through advocacy and developing cross-sectoral programmes that include aspects of economic and social development. Thus its strategy exemplifies that of mainstreaming in development described in this book.

PACT is an American organization based in Washington DC and with offices throughout Africa, South-east asia, Peru and Nepal. It has 30 years of experience working with networks of NGOs and civil society organizations. PACT has also had a long history of working with AIDS support organizations, but the increasing impact and devastation of the HIV/AIDS epidemic in Africa motivated the organization to find a way to expand its efforts and broaden its approach. PACT's AIDS Corp was created to help other NGOs and community organizations address HIV/AIDS, especially those with no prior experience in HIV/AIDS. As of September 2000, PACT had convened two meetings with a network of over 100 individuals and organizations. Religious leaders, representatives of pharmaceutical companies and academics were also invited to these meetings.

PACT has developed country strategies for specific African countries, focusing initially on Ethiopia, Zambia, Zimbabwe, Mozambique and Madagascar.

To date, the project is too new to have yielded any significant evaluation results.

From the point of view of the organization itself, its staff believes that mainstreaming HIV/AIDS work into social and economic development programmes is necessary since the epidemic is far from being exclusively a health concern. However, they have at times found it difficult for others to accept their role in HIV given that they have no established expertise. They have also encountered resistance to their support of integrated funding through cross-sectoral approaches, particularly from those concerned about diverting resources away from projects already underway. The latter tend to argue that unless HIV/AIDS budgets are separately earmarked, they will diminish. These challenges exemplify many of the problems that have plagued efforts to integrate HIV/AIDS into broader development programmes.

Case Study 8   The AIDS Support Organization (Uganda). An evolution of scaling-up strategies

The efforts of staff of The AIDS Support Organization (TASO) in Uganda to increase the scale of its activities and widen its impact could be represented as an evolution of scaling-up strategies as presented in this book. Their changing strategies reflected their response to the rapidly expanding epidemic and evolving policy context, and therefore emerging needs in the external environment, as well as their own institutional learning of what strategies were effective and manageable.

At its inception, TASO focused on sensitizing healthcare personnel to the needs of people suffering from HIV/AIDS and providing clinical services to them, as well as counselling for HIV/AIDS clients and their families.

Initial approaches to scaling up focused on strategy 1, organizational expansion, or what they refer to as 'purposive duplication'. By 1990, TASO had opened seven centres in seven out of 45 districts in Uganda.

Shortly after its inception, TASO staff realized that clinic services were insufficient and that they were incapable of responding to increased demand and were indeed risking creating a dependency on TASO services (Antivelink et al. 1996). In the early 1990s, the TASO Community Initiatives were established after recognition of the need to help communities address HIV/AIDS at the local level. Initially piloted in a few places near Kampala, they were replicated in other sites and after 1994, the programme expanded further to Entebbe, Jinja and Mbale (Antivelink et al. 1996).

By the end of 1993, TASO was providing counselling, medical care and social support to a cumulative number of over 22 000 people with HIV/AIDS and their families (Kaleeba et al. 1997). Nonetheless, despite this substantial expansion within a span of six years, there was still continued demand for services and in 1996, TASO revised its scaling-up strategy. TASO then assumed a catalyst role (strategy 2) in moving from direct service provision to facilitating capacity-building of other organizations. Thus a network of 'TASO-like' services was created after 1996, while TASO centres continued to run as 'model HIV/AIDS care centres'. The aim of the strategy was to develop local capacity in existing health centres to provide AIDS services, medical care, counselling, family planning, sexually transmitted infection services, as well as managerial capacity.

Because TASO worked through local district committees, it was able to ensure that there was local commitment to the objectives of its organization. This strategy meant that the effective impact of TASO extended well beyond those districts where TASO services were physically located, and priority could be given to districts that lacked any type of HIV/AIDS-related services.

TASO provided limited resources to 'TASO-like services', although its own costs were more than expected because of the unanticipated need for supervision on the part of TASO staff.

An extensive participatory evaluation in 1996 prompted a revision of several of TASO's strategies for scaling up (see Antivelink et al. 1996; Kaleeba et al. 1997). Of the many lessons the organization took from the participatory review was the fact that 'HIV/AIDS is not the only issue or need in the community' (Antivelink et al. 1996) and the importance of TASO linking with organizations that address other development needs such as famine, the social and legal vulnerability of women – particularly widows – and orphans, and income generation (strategy 5).

By 1998, TASO had worked in 66 communities and trained over 2500 community volunteers. Significantly, by this time TASO was working with 41 organizations in partnerships that encompassed two hospitals, seven health centres and 32 CBOs.

Despite the tremendous success brought by this innovative approach, TASO staff recognize that their organization encountered a number of challenges in scaling up its activities, many of which have been observed among other NGOs during scaling up. These include the difficulty of monitoring the quality and extent of its services due to the lack of complete or reliable data – at least partly due to inadequate record keeping by volunteers and health workers. Their efforts were also constrained by the problem of volunteer drop out and irregular supplies of condoms and drugs. They also acknowledge the problems of having only a few trained counsellors covering a large geographic area.

As with other efforts involving collaboration with public sector staff, there were also specific challenges, such as the additional work and responsibilities placed on the staff of district health facilities when there were no financial incentives attached. Moreover, high staff turnover rates at the local health units meant that there was a continual need to train new workers.

This case study illustrates that at different points of the HIV/AIDS epidemic, and on the basis of experience accumulated by individual organizations, strategies for scaling up are likely to evolve significantly over time.

CHAPTER FIVE

Partnerships and alliances

With the possible exception of organizational expansion, all of the strategies for scaling up NGO activity in HIV/AIDS described in Chapter 4 involve some sort of relationship with other organizations. NGOs, even if they scale up their activities, cannot respond to the HIV/AIDS epidemic alone and thus need to forge relationships with governments, the private sector, community organizations and research institutions active in HIV/AIDS among other areas. Thus key questions that must be addressed would include for example: What incentives are there for the other organizations to take over or adopt the new activities? Is there compatibility between the two types of organization? Are there salary differences or unequal power relations between the different types of organization that could affect the expansion from pilot to programmes of greater scale? For example, if the initial effort is established by an NGO and then transferred to government services where civil servant salaries are lower in relation to the NGO, how can sustainability be achieved? Will the initiating organization eventually withdraw or transfer the programme to the other organization and if so, when and how? In what follows, some aspects of these questions will be examined in light of the specific relationships involved.

GOVERNMENT/NGO RELATIONS

The scope for cooperation between government and NGOs in the context of the HIV/AIDS epidemic depends on both the political context and the degree to which governments are open to such input, and whether NGOs perceive the benefit of interacting more closely with government. As the prevalence of HIV/AIDS rises rapidly, governments often look to NGOs for expertise in addressing the epidemic, and therefore may be more open to collaboration. But high prevalence is not a necessary condition for successful partnerships. Often, governments and NGOs tend to regard each other with mutual suspicion (see Figure 7), rather than seek channels of collaboration. NGOs are often frustrated by the inability of public sector delivery mechanisms to be flexible or innovative, or to respond to changing community needs. They may inevitably feel – depending on political context – that unequal power relations between government and NGOs means that the NGO is inevitably the junior partner and government 'calls the shots'. Similarly, governmental staff may be wary of involvement with NGOs whom they may regard as opportunistic and donor-driven, or representing the interests of particular social groups and not addressing the wider national picture. There is

Figure 7 Government–NGO relations: the challenges of starting a joint Ministry of Health/NGO home care programme for local NGOs/CBOs involved in HIV/AIDS

Source: Illustration used at presentation by the Cambodia Home Care Network at the Horizons/Alliance Seminar (2000).

also the view that the increasing appeal of NGOs to international donors seeking to disburse expanding budgets for HIV/AIDS may by-pass governments. Ainsworth and Teokul (2000: 58) note for example that: 'In many instances, the tendency of international agencies to work through NGOs has the effect of marginalising the government'.

Certainly mutual competition over resources, and particularly donor funding, can inhibit cooperation. Nevertheless, NGOs, even if they operate at a larger scale, cannot respond single-handedly to the HIV/AIDS epidemic and thus NGO–government partnerships are essential. As Thomas (1992) notes about NGOs in general, if NGO approaches are to be generalized, it is not realistic to do so through working in the same way in other localities, but there is a need for supportive regional and national institutions. This calls into question, then, NGOs' relationships with these other players.

There are a number of clear incentives for both governments and NGOs to foster partnerships if they both aim to increase the scale of HIV/AIDS activities. Government services have the advantage of greater coverage at relatively low cost (given low civil service salaries in most countries) but often lack the understanding of community dynamics and process approaches, and risk being overly intrusive or directive. Here, NGOs can have a key role in encouraging more participatory methods as well as influencing the content of HIV/AIDS programmes.

Governments and NGOs may complement each other in terms of access to different social groups. On the one hand, governments may have sole or better access to groups such as the military or the police, both of whom are highly relevant to HIV/AIDS, and be able to reach populations on a much larger scale than NGOs, such as through the public education system. Yet on the other hand, governments may be restricted in access to population groups engaged in illegal or stigmatized activities and have little political interest in working with the socially marginalized. One comparative advantage of NGOs lies in their ability and willingness to work with such groups.

NGOs may also have a particular contribution in broaching sensitive issues and then increasing the legitimacy of addressing this social problem, thus opening the door for government involvement. In other contexts, the fact that NGOs are active in some areas of HIV/AIDS may deter governments or let them off the hook from addressing these issues. Moreover, it should be noted that this is far from a one-way process in that not only might strategies described here influence government policy regarding the provision of public AIDS programmes, but policies can in turn have an impact on the environment in which NGOs operate as well.

Successful examples of NGO–governmental collaboration in development illustrate more broadly that strong relationships between individuals in the respective institutions are critical (Edwards and Hulme 1992), even though political exigencies may bring unanticipated changes in personnel within governmental institutions, and staff turnover is often high in NGOs.

Within the field of HIV/AIDS there have been a number of instances of successful collaboration between NGOs and government and both the difficulties they encountered and the success they achieved are instructive for others attempting a similar engagement. In Cambodia, for example, the governmental HIV/AIDS programme has greater fears of cultural resistance and is more risk averse in trying new models. But when NGOs such as KHANA and others working on home care show that a particular model can work, then the government may be more prepared to replicate it. Participants in the government–NGO collaboration for home-based care described below note that critical ingredients of its relative success are that both parties are aware of the benefits of partnership and respect and understand each other's systems and structures. In this case, the groups involved developed a joint mission statement and they operate as much as possible with full transparency (of funding and programme direction) (see Case Study 9).

The government–NGO collaboration in Cambodia also successfully avoided a problem characterizing many other community-initiated home care programmes, the failure to institutionalize connections or referrals to existing governmental health services. As Wilkinson and co-authors note: 'a home care programme which, at the onset, links grassroots organisations with existing public health services, and encourages shared ownership is more likely to achieve sustainability, impact and cost-effectiveness' (Wilkinson et al. 2000: 10). This ingredient of a particularly successful collaboration illustrates a broader theme, which is the importance of NGO programmes being linked into existing HIV/AIDS-related services and the dangers of NGOs assuming they can 'go it alone'.

In the Philippines, there has been relatively smooth NGO–government cooperation in HIV/AIDS, partly because the government recognizes that it cannot do everything – that although there is a National AIDS Plan it would take a long time to implement it

---

Case Study 9   Home Care Programme (Cambodia). A government–NGO alliance

Cambodia, a country recovering from protracted conflict, has one of the fastest-growing epidemics in the world, and yet the public services are extremely limited. The population is poor and most cannot afford access to prophylactic drug therapies. Widespread poor nutrition puts people living with HIV/AIDS at greater risk of opportunistic infections. Home care is particularly important given these conditions, the scarcity of hospital beds and the high proportion of people living with HIV/AIDS. In 1998, as part of the response to the growing HIV/AIDS epidemic, the Cambodia Ministry of Health established a partnership with a group of NGOs to develop and implement Cambodia's first HIV/AIDS home care programme. The Home Care Network Group (HCNG) includes both governmental and NGO representatives and works with a nascent community-based organization sector as well as monks from Buddhist temples in providing education and support services, counselling and nursing care to people living with HIV/AIDS in their homes and communities. Hospitals make and receive referrals to and from the network, and provide monthly medical supervision in the field. The ideas behind the project originated within the World Health Organization, and KHANA (The Khmer HIV/AIDS NGO Alliance), the linking organization of the International HIV/AIDS Alliance in Cambodia, provided leadership, and technical and financial support to the HCNG and local community groups involved in partnership with the national AIDS programme.

The home care model was initially developed through a pilot project in Phnom Penh in February 1998, which had a dual purpose: to implement home healthcare programmes and to determine sustainable ways in which NGOs and government could act in partnership. In December 1998, an evaluation of the project reported that home and community care was essential for providing a continuum of care, that the project was highly successful and recommended that it be strengthened and expanded. The number of teams associated with the HCNG had grown to ten by the year 2000, and teams in two areas of Battambang Province are adapting this home care model for use in rural areas.

The key to both the success of this home care model and the feasibility of scaling it up was the positive and collaborative relationship developed between a governmental partner, the Ministry of Health, and NGOs. Initiating such a partnership proved extremely challenging, not least because the national AIDS programme was underfunded, existing CBOs were not strong or institutionalized and 'there was a need to bridge conceptual gaps between NGOs and the public sector to build trust, and to foster understanding of the limitations and potential resources of each of the players' (Wilkinson et al. 2000: 11). As both NGO and government participants in this ultimately successful partnership argue, a critical prerequisite was that both parties recognized and respected the others' structures and systems.

The ongoing scaling up relies on the recruitment of a large number of volunteers, many of whom are people living with HIV/AIDS. Home care teams are competitively selected to ensure staff have appropriate attitudes towards people living with HIV/AIDS and are able to provide quality home care. Volunteers receive 60 hours of initial training as well as on-the-job training and receive expenses for ten days a month. Monthly network meetings provide feedback, coordination and support to the home care teams. Being from and living in the communities where they work, the volunteers are extremely well placed to understand the impact of the HIV/AIDS epidemic and to make links with other community services within the health sector and outside. While volunteers are key to the expansion of the model, there are also drawbacks. Volunteers generally work more than the ten days per month for which they receive expenses and because they live in the community they often feel they are always 'on call'. They expressed to evaluation teams the need for more training in the areas of stress management and in handling work-related situations that may threaten their personal security. There has also been a high turnover of volunteers, sometimes because they take up paid employment, but often because of illness or death.

Despite these difficulties, community response to the programme has been overwhelmingly positive, as confirmed by two external evaluations in 1998 and 2000. People living with HIV/AIDS reported that after home care visits they felt better able to look after themselves and had more positive outlooks towards the future. By focusing on better nutrition and early treatment of infections, the home care visits improved the health of people living with HIV/AIDS. Families had an improved sense of confidence, and the programme provided households with significant benefits in terms of financial and time savings.

The initiative also illustrates the close links between caring for those with HIV/AIDS, mitigating the effects of the epidemic and its prevention. By allowing people living with HIV/AIDS to remain in the community, this model of home care fosters better understanding of HIV/AIDS, correcting misunderstandings about both prevention and care as they arise, and helps to reduce discrimination against those with HIV. Community leaders in Phnom Penh mentioned to an evaluation team, for example, that until the home care team started visiting, people did not believe there was AIDS in their areas. Their visits helped to increase knowledge about HIV/AIDS and understanding of preventive measures (Wilkinson et al. 2000).

The experience of Cambodia provides an instructive example of the potential benefits of scaling up through government–NGO partnerships. As the evaluators of the programme note, the approach was particularly well suited to the context and needs of Cambodia. It remains to be seen, however, whether the model developed to serve an urban area will be suitable or will need substantial modification as the programme expands into rural areas.

fully. For example, NGOs initiated an effort to train public school teachers in HIV/AIDS, a model that the government subsequently adopted.

A number of key lessons for fostering dialogue between NGOs and government emerge from the case study of KANCO, an organization that aims to complement the government response to HIV/AIDS while at the same time ensuring a positive policy environment by lobbying government to sustain attention to HIV/AIDS. The executive director of KANCO, Allan Ragi, sits on the National AIDS Control Council, which coordinates HIV/AIDS activities in the country, to promote the perspective of Kenyan NGOs. KANCO's efforts contributed significantly to the development of the 1997 Session Paper No. 4 'AIDS in Kenya'. KANCO has also sponsored several symposia to build the capacity of members of parliament to respond to the epidemic in their constituencies. Allan Ragi notes that governments find collective networking threatening and therefore one has to actively look for opportunities to encourage the participation of government representatives and to cultivate personal relationships between NGOs and government. At the same time, governments will only respect the viewpoints and arguments of NGO coalitions if they represent the authentic views of grassroots organizations.

In Guatemala, an explicit objective of ASI's scaling up was to expand partnerships with government in order to ensure the sustainability of the project and ongoing funding. Although collaboration with the government has been relatively slow, the Ministry of Health came increasingly to seek assistance from organizations with experience as the epidemic continued to escalate.

Despite these examples of successful cooperation, relationships or collaborations with government are not always sustainable. ASI found that, having sought and developed a fruitful collaboration with government, when the government changed they had to start again and agreements made with a previous administration were not upheld. Moreover, in Cambodia – where the government finances NGOs in home-based care – financial sustainability is not necessarily assured.

As the foregoing examples make clear, attitudinal change is required on both sides of the NGO–government relationship if the prospects for greater coordination in HIV/AIDS are to be realized. But this also demands that systems and structures are in place to facilitate that collaboration. Surmounting these attitudinal and procedural barriers to greater cooperation between government and NGOs in HIV/AIDS has a potential for high returns. Ultimately, governmental services are unique in their national scope, and only governments possess full information of the situation at the national level as well as being accountable to the general public to a degree most NGOs are not.

NGO–CBO COLLABORATION

A number of successful efforts to scale up HIV/AIDS programmes have worked as a result of collaborations between professional NGOs and small CBOs. The experience of FACT/FOCUS in Zimbabwe shows how community initiatives can be strengthened and can serve as examples for other communities through partnership with NGOs who are able and willing to learn from the community experiences. Their first pilot was established in 1993 in a particular region of Zimbabwe where communities were already addressing HIV/AIDS through a church. At its inception, 19 volunteers working in 19 villages led this effort. After one year FOCUS did an evaluation and found that the programme identified the majority of orphans and targeted those most in need and most vulnerable in material terms. FACT/FOCUS then played a catalysing role to replicate the initiative in nine sites (with the number of families reached increasing from 798 to 2764). In this case, the role of the NGO FACT/FOCUS was to supervise the existing programme, by providing both technical and organizational development support, assisting with the replications by the same CBO (strategy 1, organizational expansion) and by other CBOs (strategy 2, catalyst). As Foster describes this experience, the 'light touch' style of administration demanded a great deal of trust and open com-munication between community organizations and FACT, but the benefits were two-way. Without the 'light-touch' approach, there is a danger that NGOs take over community initiatives and destroy a nascent support structure rather than nurturing it. As Foster describes this relationship:

> *Partnerships between non-governmental and community-based organisations are mutually beneficial, enabling neighbourhood associations to develop community coping mechanisms while at the same time permitting external partners to gain better understanding and document these mechanisms by learning through the decisions and experiences of community members.*

> *(Foster et al. 1996: 401)*

There is a converse risk, however, that in relying solely on community initiatives there may be reluctance to address marginal social groups or sensitive issues. In this case, the external agency may need to intervene to counter this resistance, while at the same time not undermining exist-ing momentum. The Family Health Trust in Zambia faced this dilemma when it found that the Anti-AIDS Clubs tended to exclude young girls.

Another potential drawback of many such partnerships is the failure to ensure that the community initiatives are sufficiently linked into health and other service structures, whether public, private or charity based. There is a danger that the effort may stimulate demand for services or commodities on a scale that cannot be met. If a continuum of interventions – from prevention to care and support – is to be provided, fostering these links in advance of expansion is particularly critical, as is addressed in the next section.

NGO–HEALTH SERVICES COLLABORATION

A number of NGO approaches to scaling up – whether entailing strategy 2 (catalyst), 3 (diffusion) or 4 (influencing policy) – have specifically sought alliances with existing health services provided by the public or private sector or by other NGOs. ASI, an NGO provid-ing health services related to HIV/AIDS in Guatemala, found that as the scope of the epidemic increased, the importance of alliances with other healthcare providers became more evident. In 1996–97, ASI ran the only clinic in Guatemala offering integrated services to people living with HIV/AIDS, and the organisation's staff felt that it needed to convince other institutions to offer similar services. Thus they actively sought alliances with other health providers to encourage this approach. ASI further benefited from insights concerning quality of care through their strategic alliances with staff at another hospital with whom they coordinated care through weekly meetings. They also collaborated with a large service provided by social security, which had an even higher level of patient load than ASI and whose staff were able to offer assistance with protocols for treatment. These protocols – developed by an infectious disease specialist associated with public and private institutions – were then given to the National AIDS programme for their approval.

Similarly, the experience described earlier of establishing a home-based care programme in Cambodia profited from the fact that a good relationship has developed between the home-based care model and hospitals. At the same time, the hospitals sometimes refuse referrals from the home care teams for various reasons. This suggests that just as CBOs may have to be encouraged to reach out to include marginalized communities, hospitals may also have to be encouraged to include people living with HIV/AIDS. This case illustrates the potential role of NGOs lobbying for policy changes to facilitate treatment of people living with HIV/AIDS and their role in reducing the legitimacy of discrimination.

Even where the approach to scaling up does not entail a direct link with health services, one measure of the effectiveness of the scaling up may be whether it stimulates greater demand for and reduces the stigma associated with seeking care from formal health services. In this case, the information available from the health services may be valuable. For example, in evaluating whether the Zambian Anti-AIDS Clubs AIDS education messages were effective, staff from that organization used data from health services to analyse whether more young people were using the services.

At the same time, as noted above, NGO activities may raise demand for health services that are not sufficiently accessible or unprepared for the greater utilization, thus creating unrealistic expectations. In the Cambodian example, the participation of staff from the understaffed and supplied health centres in the home care visits may take them away from other functions. And TASO in Uganda found that its activity as an NGO often stimulated greater demand for public services, and there was a constant struggle to work with those services to help them to respond to the increased need for them.

Both macro-economic structural adjustment programmes and health sector reform programmes implemented under new procedures for disbursing assistance for health in developing countries – known as sector-wide approaches – may alter the pattern of NGOs' relations with governmental health services. These, in turn, could shape the scaling-up approaches that NGOs active in HIV/AIDS adopt. To date, there has been little research on how sector-wide approaches are affecting work on HIV/AIDS. Certainly many of the constraints to scaling up that NGOs have experienced, as documented in this book, relate to wider systematic deficiencies in the healthcare system as a whole. In the case of TASO, as well as of the Cambodian home-based care programme, low salaries and high turnover at the governmental health services were key constraints to the sustainability of the partnership. Similarly, the inability of NGOs to access commodities as they expand the scale of their activities is a deficiency cited widely by NGOs that have attempted to do so. The greatest difficulty PSG experienced as it scaled up relates to the limited access to commodities such as STI treatment, home-care medicine, food and condoms, particularly as needs grow.

There is some evidence that health sector reform may, at least in the short to medium term, constrain budgets and strain the infrastructure available for work on HIV/AIDS. One study on home-based care in Zambia notes that, for example: 'In the past, the government provided drug kits to home-based care projects through the WHO. Since the introduction of health reforms, this support has ceased' (Nsutebu et al. 2001: 244).

In Cambodia, the implications of the newly implemented health sector reform for the work of the home care teams are not yet clear. For the purposes of the reform, the country has been divided into 73 districts, each of which has a referral hospital. These are supposed to support health centres and to provide a minimum package of activities and drugs. Whether this will help or constrain the work of the home-care teams described above is not evident. Moreover, there does not seem to be a coherent strategy for prioritizing districts to ensure referral is improved or service delivery expanded.

In some instances, NGOs may be better equipped – for example with drugs and other HIV/AIDS-related commodities – than their governmental counterparts, thus making NGO–government relations difficult and raising serious ethical questions. In the case of Cambodia, the public sector is still weak and under-resourced as the country recovers from prolonged conflict, and in many cases the international NGOs are running services that are much better supplied and managed than the governmental services. There is a risk that NGOs effectively create parallel systems. Again, this and other instances of tensions or strained relationships point to the need for NGOs to seek collaboration with governmental health services and to analyse their own comparative advantage in the larger national picture.

NGO–RESEARCH COLLABORATION

A number of examples of successful scaling up efforts by NGOs emerged out of collaborations with research institutions. The added benefit of this type of partnership is the opportunity to build rigorous research and evaluation capacity into the NGO effort. For example, the PSG in Zimbabwe evolved from a University of Zimbabwe research project into a service-delivery organization. Staff at the university had been conducting an ethnographic study of HIV-vulnerable low-income women in Bulawayo, Zimbabwe, and the women who participated in the study requested STD/HIV/AIDS education and services (Case Study 1). Research continues to inform the PSG programmes, although as their activities have expanded in three Southern African countries, they note a continual challenge entailed in maintaining the quality of their research.

In some cases, organizations find that there is particular value in affiliations to outside training and research institutions if national capacity in that particular area does not exist. SIAAP, in its diffusion of the concept of community counselling, cooperated with a number of European institutions with expertise in that area, since the concept was not known in India. This helped to increase the legitimacy of this field. And as noted earlier, ASI enlists medical students to assess the quality of its interventions.

While it is undeniable that HIV/AIDS-related NGOs which integrate research or originate with a research project, such as was the case for the PSG in Zimbabwe, tend to pay greater attention to measuring and documenting their impact, there are also drawbacks to this approach. The first concerns the time frame of the initiative. Frequently, research – and the funding on which it is based – is time limited, whereas preventing and mitigating the HIV/AIDS epidemic has necessarily a much longer-term time horizon. There may be academic or financial pressures associated with research to demonstrate the effectiveness of an intervention within a short time frame, say of two to three years. One that has succeeded during this interval may not have the sustainability to endure over the long term. Indeed, it is arguable that it is specifically because of their measurability and suitability to research that short-term interventions have dominated approaches to the epidemic.

The second potential drawback of a scaling-up process beginning with, or being oriented to, research pertains to issues of accountability. Researchers are often more answerable to their respective academic institutions than to the constituencies who are the subject of their investigations. While there is a wide continuum in the degree to which researchers engage local stakeholders and ensure that their research findings translate into improvements on the ground, this danger persists.

NGO–PRIVATE SECTOR COLLABORATION

Increasingly, NGOs are seeking alliances with companies and the private sector generally in the implementation of their scaling-up programmes. Corporate funding for NGO programmes is also increasing (the implications of which will be discussed in more detail in Chapter 8). NGOs that initiate relationships with companies or business tend to work as policy advisors, service providers or in educating businesses about HIV/AIDS, although increasingly NGOs are involved in lobbying for general changes in business policy on issues such as employment rights for individuals with HIV/AIDS and drugs pricing policies adopted by pharmaceutical companies (UNAIDS 2000a). In so doing they have drawn public attention to the critical issues and policy implications of HIV/AIDS in the workplace. Many of the successful examples relate to the involvement of NGOs in the scaling up of private sector activities, rather than the other way around.

The International HIV/AIDS Alliance has actively sought out relationships with the corporate sector as one partner in the multi-faceted response to the HIV/AIDS epidemic.[23] It has done so at an international level as well as in its support for linking organizations, which have, for example, worked with garment factories in Bangladesh and oil companies in Ecuador. Alliance staff recognize that this strategy has both benefits and challenges. Benefits include

access to financial resources, greater understanding of the pharmaceutical industry and business sector, access to decision-makers and
information sharing. From their experience, the risk that business
agendas may be imposed on NGOs is real, but this is true of other
donors as well. Thus it is critical to maintain a broad and diverse
funding base.

Particularly successful examples of efforts to foster NGO–business
partnerships can be found in Thailand. There, the Thai Business
Coalition on AIDS, a business-membership NGO, aims to increase
the scale of its impact by increasing the involvement of business
leaders in workplace AIDS programmes and to guide the development of AIDS policies in business settings (Sittitrai 1994). In 1999, an
alliance between American International Assurance, Thailand (a
branch of the American International Group, a US-based international insurance organization) and the Thai Business Coalition on
AIDS aimed to provide credit premium value to companies implementing HIV/AIDS policies and education programmes in the workplace.[24] The alliance aims to provide financial incentives to
companies to promote prevention and reduce discrimination in the
workplace. Companies will be rewarded with a 5–10% credited premium value group life insurance on the basis of evaluation of their
programmes on entry to the programme and once before the yearly
renewal of the policy. Thus the programme incorporates a mechanism to measure whether concrete change has occurred. The cost to
American International Assurance, Thailand of this programme in
1999 was approximately $85 000, which included the development
costs. The partners have recognized that companies need technical
capacity to undertake such HIV/AIDS programmes and thus further
alliances with governmental and NGOs specialized in HIV/AIDS
have been encouraged.

It is probably fair to say that the ultimate motivation of many private companies in seeking out alliances with NGOs active in
HIV/AIDS is usually commercial (even where the immediate objective may be to counter a negative image or improve their marketing).
Nevertheless, if NGOs are to adopt the philosophy of exploiting all
possible avenues for expanding their impact on the escalating epidemic, it is opportune for them to seek such alliances. Moreover, as
we have seen with the impact of the global advocacy of NGOs on the
policies of multinational corporations and the World Trade Organization on access to antiretroviral drugs, NGOs may wield strong
influence on the policies and orientation of the private sector.

As the above examples of successful collaboration in HIV/AIDS make clear, NGO partnerships may be essential in whichever scaling-up strategy NGOs adopt. There is now increasing recognition – on the part of both NGOs and donors – that NGOs acting alone are not likely to make a dent in the epidemic, in terms of either preventing it or mitigating its effects, particularly in high-prevalence countries. Moreover, partnerships with government and health services provided by a range of institutions are often essential if a continuum of interventions from prevention to care and support is to be available. But such collaborations necessarily require time to develop, and each partner has to establish their reputation and legitimacy in the eyes of the other. They also pose questions of ownership and accountability. As Annie Hirschmann of ASI notes, this inevitably means that NGOs need to anticipate slower processes. The rewards, as the successful examples of collaboration described in this chapter illustrate, are potentially high.

CHAPTER SIX

Why and when to scale up

THE IMPORTANCE OF CONTEXT

All the strategies described in Chapter 4 that NGOs have used to scale up their HIV/AIDS programmes on the continuum from prevention to care and support are necessarily contingent on the context in which the organization finds itself operating. NGOs are often well placed to understand the social dynamics underlying vulnerability to HIV/AIDS and to be in a position to identify individuals or households in need of care and support. Yet much of the discussion of 'context' in the international literature on HIV/AIDS focuses almost exclusively on the level of the epidemic, ignoring the specificity of the social, cultural and political context. The latter shapes not only the evolution of the epidemic, but also the responses to it and thus the feasibility of scaling up such responses. Therefore a self-conscious analysis of the context in which NGOs operate and of their comparative advantage should inform NGOs' scaling-up strategies.

Part of the reason for this lack of attention to context has been the premium value placed at the international level in HIV/AIDS on establishing knowledge or the 'evidence base' for selected interventions in HIV/AIDS. The so-called 'gold standard' for testing such effectiveness are randomized controlled trials, which seek to determine whether certain medical interventions are effective in a manner that is independent of the context in which they are introduced. Less attention has been paid to how these interventions can be best implemented in countries with weak capacity and frequently unstable political and economic climates. Moreover, there has been relatively little discussion in the literature about the comparative advantages of different actors within the HIV/AIDS field and their inter-relationship, particularly as programmes are scaled up. Yet, most of the interventions NGOs are engaged in are premised on recognition of the multifaceted impact of the epidemic and that both vulnerability to HIV/AIDS as well as responses to it are rooted in people's lives and social relations. NGOs are therefore more likely than other actors in HIV/AIDS to address social aspects of the epidemic – including very context-specific norms associated with gender relations, different types of sexual behaviour or the stigma associated with sexuality and death. Thus the effectiveness and feasibility of scaling up interventions implemented by NGOs in particular to address HIV/AIDS are likely to be highly context-specific. This is not to suggest, however, that NGOs cannot derive lessons from models or experiences of scaling up elsewhere.

Particularly important in determining how conducive the environment is to scaling up NGO programmes in HIV/AIDS is the policy context – both in general, in terms of such factors as relationships between state and civil society, and also specifically concerning HIV/AIDS. Of paramount importance is where the official government position on the HIV/AIDS epidemic lies on a continuum from complete denial to mainstreaming HIV/AIDS across all areas of development. Government leadership has been shown to be critical in such countries as Uganda, where high-level acknowledgement of the dangers posed by the HIV/AIDS epidemic can set the tone and motivation for constructive action across the spectrum of institutions active in that field. However, other critical elements of the policy context include the extent of state capacity, its accountability to public demands or the degree of transparency with which it governs. Political considerations would reflect the degree to which NGOs are given some autonomy within which to operate and the scope available for community organizing without fear of repression. Even adverse political contexts do not necessarily mitigate against scaling-up efforts (Myers 1992; Sittitrai 1994; Smith and Colvin 2000). Indeed, where governments are incapacitated for various political reasons – as in situations marked by complex emergencies (such as in countries recovering from prolonged civil conflict) – NGOs may find valuable opportunities for initiating activities at a greater scale. In these contexts, where governments are unlikely to be able to implement policies even if they were able to adopt them, the best option is neither to influence policy nor to mainstream HIV into development (strategies 4 and 5). Rather what may be required is careful and low-key efforts to catalyse other organizations (strategy 2) and to diffuse community-based approaches to HIV/AIDS prevention, voluntary counselling and testing as well as care and support for those affected (strategy 3).

Given the sensitivity of HIV/AIDS, cultural considerations will dictate the degree of taboo surrounding the discussion of sex generally and the stigma associated with particular sexual orientations (such as homosexuality) or sexual activity (such as sex work), as well as with injecting drug use and other potentially high-risk behaviours. Social norms and values concerning appropriate gender roles and the relative power of women and men to negotiate sexual relations may pose some of the single greatest barriers to scaling up HIV/AIDS interventions.

Another key contextual parameter that can constrain or enhance NGO scaling-up efforts is the capacity (both physical and in terms of human resources) in the country concerned. Capacity might include in this sense the strength of the health system, the availability of government infrastructure and the degree to which government provides a minimum safety net for its citizens. This, of course, will in turn be affected by the economic situation prevailing in the country and the adoption of macro-economic policies such as structural adjustment, which may severely constrain budgetary resources. Where economic or logistical constraints interrupt the supply of commodities, such as treatment for opportunistic infections or condoms, even the most successful models of scaling up can be hampered. Both the PSG in Zimbabwe and TASO in Uganda found that their potential success was limited by the lack of provision by other agencies – of condoms in the case of PSG and access to services in the case of TASO. If capacity is very low, it is likely that there will be a ceiling to efficiency gains through expansion and at a certain scale of delivery. Further investment in capacity and infrastructure will be necessary in order to be able to expand activities and exploit potential economies of scale (Kumaranayake 2000). Where state capacity and willingness to address HIV/AIDS are both low, strategies of scaling up may focus on the NGO sector alone, rather than building bridges with government services.

The feasibility of delivering scaled-up interventions will also be conditioned by the intervention context and how difficult it is to reach population groups, both in terms of social and physical access. Thus, in countries that have a relatively low level of urbanization and in which populations are dispersed in remote rural areas, or among migrant communities, scaling up is likely to be both resource- and time-intensive. In Cambodia, for example, the population remains unsettled after prolonged conflict, and the borders remain porous, making HIV-related activities all the more difficult.

Certainly, however, the above emphasis on the political and social context in which scaling up occurs is not to underestimate the significance of the epidemiological context, including both the stage and dynamics of the epidemic. Indeed, this parameter is likely to condition the other factors, such as the political will to address HIV/AIDS. Where, for example, the epidemic is not significantly advanced into the general population, and governments may still be in denial, there are not likely to be many NGOs active in HIV/AIDS either on the prevention side or in care and support. Those that do exist are likely to be impeded in their access to communities and to the mass media. This is the case in Egypt, for example, where despite significant capacity and a relatively good health infrastructure, there are few NGOs active in HIV/AIDS.[25] Thus, partnerships may need to be fostered with organizations active in development to a greater extent, or through other entry points, such as reproductive health or gender issues. In some contexts, the fact of government denial or inaction may provide a window of opportunity for NGOs. In Ecuador, precisely because the government does so little in HIV/AIDS, many NGOs were created to respond to some of the needs of people living with HIV/AIDS. Nevertheless, despite the importance of the level of the epidemic, NGOs do not always articulate different strategies according to whether their countries or areas have high or low prevalence of HIV/AIDS. As a result, the links between the relevant choice of strategies and the stage of the epidemic is usually missing from NGO and donor discussion and planning.

Another contextual parameter that NGOs need to be explicit about addressing before scaling up their programmes is their motivation for doing so, which is the topic of the following section.

MOTIVATIONS FOR SCALING UP

Within the literature on scaling up NGO efforts, there has been remarkably little attention paid to the motivation behind scaling up,[26] with the greatest emphasis being placed on the circumstances in which NGOs are pushed into increasing the scale of their efforts in order to satisfy donors who make funding available specifically for this purpose. In practice, there are a range of reasons that might motivate an NGO to scale up all or some of its programmes.

Expansion may be externally induced if the overall context in which NGOs operate changes, either because of the evolution of the

HIV/AIDS epidemic itself (as it expands rapidly and/or extends into other social groups or geographic areas, for example) or the natural history of the disease (with increasing proportions of the beneficiary community becoming symptomatic). For example, in the face of a rapidly increasing epidemic in Guatemala, ASI decided that it should either expand substantially or close. The overall policy climate may change, either in a negative or positive direction due to changes in government stances regarding HIV/AIDS, or the activities of other organizations. Alternatively, the beneficiaries of an organization may be the driving force behind expansion. They may demand a greater scale in terms of the numbers of persons reached, geographic areas covered or the type of activities undertaken. In many cases, increasing the scale of activities is part of a deliberately conceived research process, beginning with a pilot study and involving a staged programme of expansion. The PSG, as noted previously, began as an ethnographic study in the University of Zimbabwe, and subsequently moved into service delivery. Research continues to inform its ongoing programme.

In other instances, the introduction of new technologies – such as the female condom or microbicides – may drive efforts to expand the scale or types of NGO programmes. International pressure and advocacy or the evolution of ideas at the international level often play a key role in inspiring certain forms of expansion. As was evident at the International Conference on Population and Development, when a particular approach – such as integrating HIV/AIDS within reproductive healthcare – is endorsed at the international level, this can play a very influential role in the design of local programmes. However, the extent to which such integration is indeed desirable and is actually happening remains debatable (Mayhew 1996). Some argue that integrating HIV/AIDS into reproductive health services, which in most countries cater mainly to women, may stigmatize those services and also fail to reach men. Nevertheless, there is a strong argument that particularly in medium- to high-prevalence settings, there is a need to expand the scale of all possible HIV/AIDS interventions, and efforts should be made to integrate them into all available services. Failure to do so loses valuable opportunities for reaching women with information, counselling and services.[27] Appropriate training for staff of existing health services reaching women is required, however, for them to be equipped and sensitized to deal with the special issues of HIV/AIDS in women.

The desire for expansion may have little to do with external factors but rather be entirely internally motivated, either at the initiative of a visionary and charismatic leader or through staff consensus. Expansion may stem from observed success in smaller-scale activities and the desire to expand this effort. Alternatively, it may be driven internally, at times by the discovery of obstacles to successful programmes. For example, the Self Employed Women's Association in Ahmedabad, India – a trade union with a membership of over 200 000 women – developed to represent the economic interests of disadvantaged women, but expanded into health when staff found that the main reasons for defaults on loans were maternal mortality and health problems.

Personal motivation, such as a desire for professional advancement, social recognition or prestige, may also provide the underlying impetus to programme expansion. In many cases, leaders of organizations stake their careers on the visibility, influence and indeed size (as measured in numbers of employees or in overall budgets) of the organizations they direct. The notion that NGOs need to increase in size in order to compete with other organizations for donor funding or influence is widely held. As Jeff O'Malley of the International HIV/AIDS Alliance notes: 'It is rare indeed for an NGO of any size to conclude that it is doing enough, or that it has enough resources.' The implications of this kind of subjective motivation both for staff and the organization itself are complex, however, and this impact will depend on the nature of the NGO and the context in which it is operating.

The type of factor motivating the scaling-up process will, to a large extent, dictate whether the initiating organization perceives itself to be able to steer the process, as opposed to being driven by forces beyond its control. Especially in the context of HIV, NGOs can feel that they are obliged to take on other activities because of overwhelming poverty and the lack of services in the face of a devastatingly rapid spread of the epidemic. In these circumstances, the lack of time, opportunity or resources to prepare for scaling up can have a detrimental effect on its ultimate effectiveness. In other situations where control is equally lacking, where expansion is induced by the exigencies of foreign funding, for example, scaling up may actually dilute effectiveness.

Similarly, selecting which strategy from those delineated in the typology presented in Chapter 4 may not be a result of free choice, and indeed organizations may resort to certain strategies rather than others as a compromise. Where funding is not available for the NGO's own growth, or to catalyse other organizations (strategy 2), some might resort to policy advocacy with both government and donors in order to encourage them to provide the necessary funds to support grassroots activities.

TO SCALE UP OR NOT?

As the preceding chapters have illustrated, arguments for scaling up HIV/AIDS activities are strong on moral, epidemiological and cost-effectiveness grounds. Nonetheless, this should not be interpreted to mean that all institutions should scale up their activities or that all activities should be scaled up. The impact of many excellent small-scale programmes has been through the dissemination of their project experiences rather than scaling up itself (Boyce et al. 1997: 383). Most countries have and need a diversity of types and sizes of organization active in HIV/AIDS, which are complementary to each other. Thus both NGOs and government need to be clear about their own comparative advantage within this larger national picture. Moreover, not all organizations or activities are ready for scaling up, either in terms of financial capacity, internal organizational characteristics or programme maturity. Boyce and his co-authors, in reviewing the scaling up of rehabilitation programmes, found that it is often older organizations which are best prepared to scale up, given that they have established reputations and have the requisite community links (Boyce et al. 1997). In the relatively new field of HIV/AIDS, 'programme maturity' needs to be seen in relative terms.

A set of 'preconditions' proposed by Baba Goumbala of ANCS in Senegal (see Figure 8) is a good starting point for a discussion of how the internal landscape of an NGO can influence a decision on whether or not to scale up.

Each of these preconditions is open to debate. Many NGOs would probably agree that to link scaling up to the 'rhythm' of the community may be too restricting, since many issues which are key to addressing HIV may be disregarded, ignored or simply not be understood if the community is without some external influence. Thus there may be an inherent conflict between the 'rhythm' of the NGO and that of the community or communities concerned, and there is often a necessary role for outside agencies to stimulate action related to these sensitive concerns or marginalized social groups.

Many NGOs have found themselves scaling up without adequate planning and even without taking a conscious decision to do so, in

- Evaluation is necessary before expansion

- The desire and willingness to do more and better must come from inside the NGO and not be imposed from outside

- The NGO must have the resources and capacity appropriate to the scaling up

- The scaling up should be initiated at the NGO's own rhythm and at the rhythm of the community

- The NGO must control the know-how and direction of the scaling-up transition process

Figure 8   Six preconditions for scaling up
Source: Goumbala, Baba, ANCS, Senegal.

response to external stimulation or growing demand for their services. But where NGOs do deliberately decide to initiate scaling-up processes, three elements must be taken into consideration to ensure that the organization is sufficiently prepared. The first is that time and resources are devoted to planning for the scaling-up process. The second is that organizations analyse their own comparative advantage within the larger picture of activities within the HIV/AIDS sector. Third, the institution must consider the internal implications of scaling up for leadership, management, staffing, structure and costs. The latter internal dimensions will be further addressed in the final section of this book, whereas the focus here is on questions of strategy and effectiveness.

A number of programmatic questions must be addressed before the scaling-up exercise begins (see Figure 9). These include the question of *who* to focus on, both in terms of the beneficiaries of interventions, as well as whether the scaling-up exercise would be confined to the original organization (strategy 1) or work with other institutions – NGO, private or governmental (strategies 2–5). For example, should the scaling up of prevention activities focus on increasing the numbers of people reached in absolute terms, or concentrate on those most likely to affect the dynamics of the epidemic, or perhaps most likely to adopt behavioural changes? Similarly, in terms of scaling up care and support initiatives, what criteria should be used to target or prioritize beneficiaries?

Feasibility as determined by:		
Contextual parameters	*Institution-specific considerations*	*Intervention-specific considerations*
Overall political context	Time to plan scaling up	Aim of scaling up this
Government–NGO relations	Resources available to	intervention
Government position on	plan and implement	Who (what groups) to
HIV/AIDS	Analysis of own	focus on?
Stability versus conflict	comparative advantage	What level of coverage
Level of epidemic	in HIV/AIDS	will be sought?
Characteristics of	Internal implications	What (interventions) to
epidemic	(staffing,	focus on?
Ease of reaching	management etc.)	Evidence for effectiveness
populations	Capacity to implement	of interventions
Economic context	and evaluate programme	Evaluation mechanism
Available infrastructure		– to measure quality
		and impact of
		intervention
		Costs of intervention:
		scaling-up
		strategy
		Sustainability of
		scaling-up process

Figure 9   Strategic questions NGOs need to ask before scaling up

Some NGOs have successfully scaled up their prevention programmes by focusing on the groups most vulnerable to HIV/AIDS.
PSG explicitly targets low-income communities and people who
are particularly vulnerable to HIV infection. Similarly, the Healthy
Highways Project in India – an initiative of the UK Department for
International Development and the Government of India, including a
number of NGO partners such as the Naz Foundation – specifically
targets truck drivers (and their partners) as being most vulnerable to
HIV/AIDS because of their mobility (see Case Study 13).

Such an approach based on epidemiological notions of risk is often
highly effective, but may tend to narrow emphasis on the target
groups without looking sufficiently at their partners or the circumstances governing their sexual behaviour. The approach of the
Healthy Highways Project has been exceptional. As Allan Ragi of
KANCO notes about similar programmes targeting truck drivers in

Africa, they have often neglected groups such as the partners of the truck drivers or the secretaries in the companies for which they work.

Following a social model of health, and endeavouring to understand the social processes driving the epidemic, may lead to HIV/AIDS NGOs putting more emphasis on groups likely to bring about social change – that is, 'vectors of social change' rather than the 'vectors of the epidemic'. SIAAP chose to work with an innovative target group of blind people. On epidemiological criteria alone, this may not seem an effective group to focus on given their relatively small population size.[28] The facts that the blind are particularly disadvantaged in gaining access to HIV/AIDS material (most of which is written) or that they may be more stigmatized than most when purchasing condoms make this an important group to focus on in social terms, if the objective is to counter stigma associated with HIV/AIDS.

NGOs addressing HIV have mainly been involved with service provision or, increasingly over the past few years, organizational capacity development and technical support for local organizations. More attention is being paid to the concept of human capacity development, and the ways in which individuals, through community and organizational relationships, work across cultural and organizational barriers to create an environment which facilitates change at local and community level. Some NGOs, including the Salvation Army and FACT/FOCUS, have worked with this approach at local and international level. Scaling up in this context does not necessarily involve increasing the size or capacity of an organization itself. This is a complementary approach to service provision, based on the capacity of people to respond, rather than on the provision of technological solutions and technical support.

If the aim of scaling up by taking this approach is to extend indigenous community initiatives, then it is important to understand how to stimulate spontaneous links between and among communities. The orphan support programmes that FACT/FOCUS has supported expanded, through links between church groups, to other communities (see Case Study 10).

The second key question is *what* to focus on in scaling up in terms of particular HIV/AIDS activities. This in turn will depend on a number of dimensions, such as the *feasibility* of particular strategies – including technical aspects and questions of access to necessary resources (such as condoms or pharmaceuticals), costs as well as political considerations.

Case Study 10   The Family AIDS Caring Trust/Family, Orphans and Children Under Stress (Zimbabwe). Encouraging community initiatives in HIV/AIDS

The gradual scaling up of a programme to support orphans and children under stress due to HIV/AIDS in Zimbabwe, described here, illustrates a community-initiated effort that spread spontaneously to other areas. The NGO's role was to catalyse and strengthen that transfer or spread. Along with the case study on the Anti-AIDS Clubs, this experience lends weight to arguments that every effort should be made to investigate community coping mechanisms dealing with the HIV/AIDS epidemic and to scale up through supporting them.

Family AIDS Caring Trust (FACT) is a Zimbabwean NGO established in Mutare by a visionary individual in 1987. It works with a variety of NGOs and CBOs to promote quality HIV/AIDS interventions. In 1991, FACT's director, Dr Geoff Foster, was alarmed at the growing number of malnourished orphans he encountered during his work as a paedia-trician at a government hospital. FACT then sponsored a study to count the number of orphans in a target area, look at how communities and extended families were coping with HIV/AIDS, and determine how best to support their efforts.

The first programme of Family, Orphans and Children Under Stress (FOCUS), which works primarily with church-based CBOs to provide support to children affected by AIDS, began through the initiative of members of a church near Mutare. FACT employed an orphan pro-gramme coordinator based in Mutare who was responsible for estab-lishing, maintaining and documenting the FOCUS programme. The coordinator provided training (about AIDS, orphan enumeration, needs assessment and care of orphans) to the community volunteers, as well as administrative support through site visits. The training was participa-tory in style, since many of the visitors were elderly and semi-literate (Foster et al. 1996).

Because this initiative was community-led, it was able to capitalize on local knowledge of needs in relation to HIV/AIDS. After one year, an evaluation found that the group of volunteer visitors had successfully identified a large population of orphans in the target area, prioritizing the most needy households and mobilizing community members to provide regular visits and support to these households. Using local knowledge, therefore, the community visitors were able to implement an informal but accurate targeting system. The evaluation found that the programme identified 14.7% of children in the target area as orphans, while a formal orphan enumeration of 248 randomly selected households carried out in 1992 in the same district found that 17.2% of children were orphans (Foster et al. 1996).

The scaling-up process of this early effort was largely spontaneous and through community initiatives – as other churches heard about the success of the pilot project they asked FACT, the facilitating NGO, to help them establish similar programmes. Local leaders and pastors saw tangible benefits being provided to those in need and sought to establish the programme in their own communities. FOCUS thus evolved to work with church-based groups in a wider geographic area to provide support to children affected by AIDS. Its staff identify households where children's basic needs are unmet and help develop a sustainable plan to improve their quality of life. By 1998, FACT supervised nine FOCUS sites with 178 volunteers providing regular visits to 2764 orphan households.

Throughout the scaling-up process FACT/FOCUS staff deliberately worked at the pace of the local volunteers involved and made every effort to foster community ownership of the initiative. As a result, there was little dilution of the strength of the original model as the scaling up proceeded. The effort was more sustainable than externally supported orphan support programmes which often run the risk of undermining community coping mechanisms by initiating activities or providing material support without sufficient community participation (Foster et al. 1996).

Reduction in material support and supervision provided by FACT to FOCUS sites encouraged the CBOs to become more autonomous. One CBO obtained external funding and was able to employ its own staff and develop a board of directors, thus becoming an NGO in its own right. A second evaluation conducted in 1999 indicated that FOCUS programmes enjoyed high levels of volunteer retention and sense of community ownership.

As needs increased with rising HIV prevalence in Zimbabwe, and the demand for similar programmes arose in other areas, FACT staff recognized the need for both internal change in management style as well as new models of offering support to local volunteers. Attempts were made to increase collective decision-making and to encourage site supervisors to become more involved in planning activities and budgeting. This enabled FACT/FOCUS staff to reduce the level of direct support and supervision.

Overall, the process of scaling up was also advantageous to FACT as an organization. The additional work involved in supervising additional FOCUS sites was compensated for by an increase in mutual support from site supervisors and volunteers. FACT was able to learn from the innovations introduced by community-based partner organizations that informed the development of further programmes.

From the perspective of the founders of the organization, the greatest challenge was finding a balance between FACT's perceived need to supervise programme sites to maintain programme quality, obtain monitoring data and understand new problems, while also ensuring that communities had sufficient autonomy to foster their own sense of ownership in the programme.

The second dimension would be the *effectiveness* of scaling up particular strategies, which points to the need for research to inform the strategies chosen. Yet NGOs often do not have the requisite information to assess effectiveness, either because they lack exposure to technical innovations or new findings or results of interventions tested elsewhere, or do not have the resources or orientation to undertake research themselves (Sittitrai 1994).

Finally, the strategy chosen would need to be based on assessment of the *capacity* of the organization (or partner organizations) to undertake the scaling up. Questions of capacity should be assessed in relation to existing capacity within both the non-governmental and governmental sectors. The internal capacity of organizations is addressed in the final section of this book.

In conclusion, NGOs need to analyse their own comparative advantage in the larger national picture before scaling up their programmes and ask themselves a number of questions (as outlined in Figure 9). The political, social and economic contexts in which they operate, as well as government policy on HIV/AIDS, are likely to be critical determinants of the success of their efforts. Self-awareness is also called for in acknowledging why a given organization is choosing to scale up. Once decisions are made to scale up, NGOs need to explore the internal implications for their institution, as well as the feasibility of the particular approaches to HIV/AIDS that are adopted. One type of information which NGOs – and those supporting them – often lack, is on the costs of scaling up. For that reason, the next chapter is devoted to presenting the ways in which economists have costed HIV/AIDS programmes and the implications of these for NGOs.

CHAPTER SEVEN

Considering cost

THE CONTRIBUTIONS AND LIMITATIONS OF COSTING STUDIES

Information on the cost implications of alternative scaling-up strategies is useful to NGOs as one criterion for making decisions about whether or not to embark on scaling up and if so, how to go about it in the context of constrained resources. However, there is a lack of work on the costing of HIV/AIDS programmes; indeed, as of the year 2000, there were only some 30 studies on costing HIV/AIDS programmes for sub-Saharan Africa (World Bank 2000). NGOs themselves often neglect to consider the cost implications of their work and as a result there is even less information about the costs of NGO programmes in HIV/AIDS. Of the 13 NGOs whose case studies are presented in this book, only three explicitly addressed cost as an inherent part of the scaling-up strategy.

The lessons that can be drawn from the existing costing literature are useful for NGOs choosing to scale up, but at the same time have limits in their application, for several reasons. First, most studies have been based on a snapshot picture at a specific time, and therefore do not capture the dynamic aspects of reaching different levels of scale. Given often unstable economic conditions in many developing countries, cost structures may, in general, be expected to change quite significantly as a result of macro-economic conditions (such as devaluation for example), and the scaling-up process itself is likely to have clear implications for costs over time. Second, strong international attention to so-called 'evidence-based interventions' has meant that such costing studies have tended to be intervention based. For example, studies have been conducted on such interventions as implementing voluntary counselling and testing, but these have often been hosted or implemented by research institutions and therefore their findings may not be generalizable to NGOs. Often such exercises are conducted in the context of randomized control trials to test the effectiveness of given interventions, and therefore again their conditions may not be widely representative of the prevailing context of the country in question or of other institutional settings. Finally, much of the economic analysis that has been applied to HIV/AIDS derives from a public health perspective as described in Chapter 2, and tends to focus on the large-scale delivery of services usually by governments or sometimes by the private sector. NGO programmes may be premised less on delivering services to a population than facilitating community responses to the epidemic or addressing difficult-to-measure social trends such as social stigma, gender inequities in sexual negotiation or employment-related discrimination. Moreover, NGOs, as shown earlier in this book, may tend to rely to a greater degree on voluntary input (such as contributions) and volunteer labour. These and other considerations will be explored further below.

From an economist's perspective, in order to cost prevention activities one would need to know the cost of achieving a specified impact on preventing new HIV infections. However, economists recognize that measuring impact and attributing it to single interventions are both problematic, for a number of reasons. First, decreased incidence of HIV/AIDS or HIV infections averted are most accurately measured through randomized clinical trials, which are expensive and rarely implemented for behavioural change interventions (Kumaranayake et al. 2000). Where HIV/AIDS incidence does decrease, this could be due to a variety of reasons other than a particular intervention, and moreover where more than one intervention is being implemented there are likely to be synergies between them, thus making attribution difficult. Economists therefore tend to use 'proxy' measures to approximate this impact. The assumed impact, then, on HIV/AIDS from an economist's perspective is often the output of an intervention. For example, they might use the number of people reached with a specific intervention or commodity (e.g. condoms). Cost is defined as the value of resources used to provide a service, and the total cost of an intervention represents the cost of all inputs used, and varies with the number of people reached.

Despite the limitations in applying costing analyses to NGO experiences of scaling up, the techniques economists apply to assessing costs of scaling up can help NGOs both to clarify their own objectives[29] and to make decisions as to how to choose the appropriate strategy for scaling up, given their often limited budgets. Moreover, donors are often influenced by such economic approaches and organizations like the Global Fund have stated one of their goals explicitly as ensuring that increased resources are spent effectively. Thus it is essential for those engaged in scaling up to understand these concepts and not be intimidated by them.

The next section presents a description, from an economist's point of view, of the main questions relating to a determination of costs of scaling up programmes in HIV/AIDS.[30] The second section addresses the difficulties involved in costing seemingly unquantifiable dimensions of NGOs' work and thus examines the challenges of generating meaningful costing analyses concerning NGO experiences of scaling up specifically. The final section of the chapter summarizes some of the lessons learned from the limited data in the case studies presented in this book on the financial and cost implications of scaling up NGO programmes.

AN ECONOMIST'S PERSPECTIVE

Understanding the concepts of cost

There are a number of issues that come to the forefront when thinking about scaling up and costs from an institutional perspective. First, the way in which an organization approaches scaling up – or the strategy it chooses – will affect the consideration of costs. The simplest form of scaling up an NGO might engage in, as documented in this book, is organizational expansion, whereby an NGO broadens the scale of its activities by expanding its coverage or reaching different geographic areas or social groups. Alternatively, scaling up may entail catalysing other organizations to enter the HIV/AIDS field or strengthen their work, influencing the overall policy context affecting the response to the epidemic or integrating HIV/AIDS activities more broadly within development institutions and programmes. Or, as indicated in Chapter 4, NGOs may use a combination of these strategies at any one time or over the course of their scaling up. While all approaches could increase coverage, the implications for costs are quite different.

To take the simplest of these forms of scaling up, organizational expansion, Figure 10 provides a basic diagram of the relationship between increasing coverage and costs. The underlying notion behind the expansion of activities is that an organization which is expanding its scale of activities is likely to have decreasing average costs (or the cost per person reached decreases) in the early stages.

Beyond a certain point, continued expansion will see an increase in cost per person reached. This is due to both organizational character- istics (such as a need for more coordination, etc.) and the character- istics of the groups being reached (such as their accessibility). Thus expansion of activities up to a certain point brings economies of scale, so improving the efficiency of delivering services. However, beyond a certain level of activity, continued expansion will lead to dis- economies of scale and an increase in the average cost per person.

The curve in Figure 10 illustrates a typical short-run relationship between average cost (AC, or the total cost per person reached) and marginal costs (MC, or the change in total cost of reaching an addi- tional person), as hypothesized by standard neoclassical economic theory. The average cost is often thought to have a U-shaped relation- ship with respect to the level of output. This reflects the fact that at relatively low levels of activity (or scale), if one increases the number of people being reached, then average costs or the cost per person reached would decrease. At higher levels of activity (or scale) average costs are thought to increase, reflecting the fact that one might need to add substantially more inputs in order to increase the number of people being reached. Figure 10 shows that marginal costs start to increase at lower levels of activity relative to average costs, reflecting the fact that marginal costs will start to increase before average costs.

When diseconomies of scale are suggested – that is, when the cost per person reached actually increases as the project is expanded –

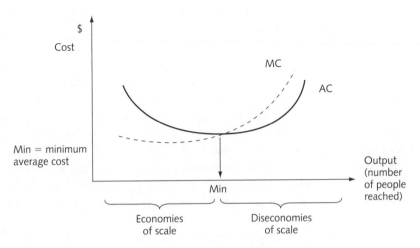

Figure 10   Relationship between average and marginal costs for a project
Source: Adapted from Kumaranayake 2000.

then cost reductions can be made by reducing the scale of activity or possibly by replicating the project (on the more efficient smaller scale) in another location. Thus, from a cost perspective, both expanding current activities or replicating projects may be desirable, depending on the actual cost structure of the project, the location where it is operating and the nature of the target population one is trying to reach.

The difficulties of measuring costs

As noted above, there is a dearth of evidence about the nature of costs in HIV/AIDS work as projects or programmes are replicated or expanded, and this is particularly true of NGOs. This is unfortunate, given the degree to which costs vary according to a wide range of criteria related to motivation, organizational characteristics and geography, among others. In a study looking at the replication of peer education interventions for HIV prevention among sex workers in Cameroon, one study found that, even within the same country, there was a two- to threefold difference in average costs across different cities, and that the cost-effectiveness varied substantially, reflecting differences in project implementation, motivation of project staff, capacity of staff to reach target populations and differences in the sex worker populations across cities (Kumaranayake et al. 2000).

A second issue related to the costs of scaling up activities lies in the nature of the resources used in a project which are directly paid for by an NGO. Financial costs represent actual expenditure on goods and services purchased. In a financial costing, costs are described in terms of how much money has been paid for the resources used. To ascertain the financial costs of a project we need to know the price and quantity of all the resources used, or alternatively the level of expenditure on these goods and services. By contrast, economic or opportunity costs recognize the cost of using resources that could have been used productively elsewhere. Thus, economic costs include the estimated value of goods or services for which there were no financial transactions (such as unpaid volunteer time) and those where the price of the goods did not reflect the cost of using it productively elsewhere (such as donated radio time) (Kumaranayake et al. 2000).

Financial costs are important when considering budgeting or cost recovery within a project. However, they may not give a full picture of the overall resources used for an activity. Economic costs are particularly useful when considering the resources needed to replicate or scale up existing activities where it may not be possible to utilize similar donated or subsidized inputs. In this case, simply using financial costs as a guide to resource requirements for scaling up may seriously underestimate the resources required. This is especially the case if there is a large proportion of inputs that are provided free, and if the proportion of these free inputs is likely to decline as activities are expanded or replicated.

For activities that have been delivered on a pilot or small scale, expansion or replication of activities may require significantly more resources than previously. This is both because of the ways in which additional services are delivered and the nature of what now has to be paid for. For example, NGOs active in HIV/AIDS frequently rely on volunteers initially, but may need to employ paid staff as the programme scales up. Or, as ASI discovered in Guatemala, scaling up which increases the numbers of volunteers may create the need to hire a paid member of staff to manage the volunteers.

THE CHALLENGE OF APPLYING COSTING ANALYSES TO NGOs' SCALING UP EXPERIENCES

The above analysis concerning the costing implications of scaling up is focused exclusively – for illustrative purposes – on the simplest strategy outlined in this book, namely organizational expansion. It is premised on a single organization and therefore does not address more challenging issues raised by the array of partnerships NGOs may forge to increase the scale of their impact. Few costing analyses exist which look at more complex and abstract strategies of scaling up, such as catalysing other organizations and diffusion of ideas or technologies, and even fewer on policy advocacy or mainstreaming in development. There is evidence, however, that the cost of interventions such as voluntary counselling and testing is lower when these programmes are integrated within existing governmental services rather than through stand-alone sites (Forsythe et al. 2002). But as the many examples throughout this book illustrate, the types of relationship NGOs engage in are varied and complex. Efforts to persuade other NGOs to enter the HIV/AIDS field, as many have done, may be a highly effective strategy particularly when recognition of the gravity of the HIV/AIDS epidemic is not widespread. However, it may also be more costly than working with NGOs with AIDS expertise, given the need for training and providing some expertise in the specific issues in the field.

Since NGOs do engage in such partnerships, any costing exercise in relation to some defined 'output' of interest would need to take into consideration that the diverse partners may have different views on the objective of the scaling up-process. For example, in the case of the partnership between SIAAP and governmental STI services in southern India, SIAAP had the objective of diffusing counselling as a practice, whereas the government saw an opportunity to increase the uptake of its services. To a certain extent, such differences in understanding of the objectives of any scaling-up initiative may apply to different levels of staff within an individual organization as well[31] and, as will be discussed in Chapter 10, often underlie tensions in donor–NGO relationships. There may also be legitimate differences of opinion – between donors and NGOs for example – as to what level of 'start-up costs' are necessary to prepare for the scaling up. As argued in Chapter 9, programmatic effectiveness is ultimately predicated upon viable institutional governance and structures, and thus these internal dimensions of scaling up need to be given due weight.

Reasons for the lack of information about costs collected by NGOs themselves no doubt relate in part to an organizational culture that does not acknowledge the importance of measuring existing and projected costs. It is also due to lack of expertise in conducting such analyses. More fundamentally, there may be a lack of consensus over the approach to measuring costs and what should be considered the most relevant 'output'. Costing analyses ultimately rely on quantifying variables to make estimates of resource requirements. This makes some uncomfortable in that many of the dimensions of success that NGOs have claimed rest on characteristics that are difficult to quantify. How does one assign a monetary value, for example, to the shared motivation of NGO staff? How can such factors as charismatic leadership be factored into costing analyses? Moreover, it may be more difficult to apply costing in areas where impact is defined more broadly and in more qualitative terms, and where the definition of scaling up is not solely based on increasing coverage or organizational expansion. For example, as illustrated in Chapter 3, the Family Health Trust's initiative to support high school Anti-AIDS Clubs in Zambia represented an exercise in scaling up which did not necessarily increase the number of people reached. Rather, it boosted the quality of an initiative that was already operating at a considerable scale.

Finally, neoclassical economic theory is premised on the maximization of utility for individuals and the maximization of profits for firms – but in the field of HIV/AIDS there is a strong role for altruism and compassion which is difficult to take into account. Assumptions of self-interested individuals exercising preferences may not apply when HIV/AIDS is a disaster affecting a region, country or particular social group. This will mean that the relationship between input and output is not a straightforward one and, as we have seen, volunteers may be motivated to work in the HIV/AIDS field without payment. While means can be found to calculate the opportunity cost by looking at the opportunities for employing that labour elsewhere, this does not provide information on the extent to which volunteer labour can be relied upon as programmes are scaled up.

LESSONS FROM THE CASE STUDIES CONCERNING COSTS

As noted at the beginning of this chapter, few of the case study organizations documented in this book addressed costs explicitly. Nevertheless, for those that did collect such data, a number of insights emerge from the case studies which are relevant to measuring the cost of scaling up HIV/AIDS programmes initiated by NGOs. They illustrate that costs are highly dynamic, varying across locations, over time and, importantly for HIV, according to the intended beneficiaries of the programme concerned. Thus costs are inherently likely to change significantly during the scaling up process. For example, the PSG initially started as a Zimbabwean initiative but gradually extended to other countries of the Southern Africa region. As indicated in Figure 11, the average costs are likely to vary substantially between countries, and indeed were found to be much higher in Zambia than in Zimbabwe for comparable interventions. Cost differences could also reflect the nature of partnerships in the two settings and who else is providing commodities or services.

Even within countries, there are often stark cost differences due to variable levels of infrastructure, the remoteness of populations and terrain, among other factors. The successful pilot project on home care developed in Cambodia, for instance, was developed in the urban area of Phnom Penh. As the scaling up proceeded it was gradually extended to rural areas where costs are much higher (as indicated in Figure 11), with resulting consequences for the finances of the NGO involved.

Location	Organizations involved	Measurement	Costs
Bulawayo, Zimbabwe	Project Support Group	Outreach meeting	US$1.20
		Cost per person reached	US$0.02
		Cost per donated condom distributed	US$0.01
Lusaka, Zambia	Project Support Group	Outreach meeting	US$7.48
		Cost per person reached	US$0.38
		Cost per donated condom distributed	US$0.05
Cambodia, urban	Cambodia Home Care Network Group	Cost per home care visit	US$9.28
Cambodia, rural		Cost per home care visit	US$14.60

Figure 11   Examples of financial unit costs presented in case studies
Note: Costs in Zimbabwe and Zambia include all expenses except for opportunity costs and donated condoms in the year 2000. Costs in Cambodia include administration, personnel and technical support costs in the year 2000. Data provided by the organizations listed.

As noted above, scaling up may result in increased average costs if one needs to introduce substantially more 'inputs' to reach increased numbers of people (see Figure 11). Indeed, there may be 'diseconomies of scale' when the cost per person reached actually increases as the project or programme is expanded beyond a certain point, rather than the often assumed 'economies of scale'. This will depend on the existing capacity of the organization initiating the activity, and whether there is potential for making increased use of existing capacity or the need to invest in new capacity. For example, as noted above, where an initial pilot project has relied on community volunteers, scaling up may call for formalizing their role within the organization, which could entail a higher, rather than lower, level of costs.

Questions of capacity and ultimately of costs also relate crucially to that of those institutions with which the organization develops partnerships in order to increase the scale of activities or coverage. As noted in Chapters 4 and 5, the majority of strategies for scaling up HIV/AIDS programmes described here rely to varying extents on key alliances with other types of institution, each of which has different cost structures. Both TASO and the Cambodia Home Care Programme case studies illustrate that the low remuneration of public sector health clinic staff (in the context of TASO's programme in Uganda) or of community workers (in the home care programme in Cambodia) can constrain the success of scaled-up programmes. In other cases, there may be an intentional decision not to remunerate community workers because of the commercial incentives this may introduce. This is illustrated by the case of PSG, which deliberately works with community volunteers and has found it is able to achieve a high level of coverage regionally in Southern Africa using this strategy. Similarly the FACT/FOCUS programmes have intentionally limited payments to community visitors to provide scope for the initiative to spread at its own pace free of distortions imposed by outside agencies, which Foster and others see as a particular risk in HIV/AIDS (Foster et al. 1996).

Organizations may make strategic choices to expand their programmes with partner institutions which, by their nature, require greater expenditure, at least initially, even though their comparative advantage of expertise makes it worth the investment to the NGO concerned. For example, the International HIV/AIDS Alliance made a strategic decision to focus its efforts largely on development organizations rather than those specializing in HIV/AIDS in most contexts where it has worked. But as the executive director of that organization notes: 'In the Alliance's initial business plan, no explicit acknowledgement was made of the very clear cost difference between supporting successful and capable organizations to expand, as opposed to convincing and supporting organizations with very little HIV/AIDS experience to begin, improve and expand work on HIV/AIDS.'

In other cases, partnerships may lead to lower costs. As the case study on the Cambodian home care programme illustrates (see Case Study 9), the strong collaboration between government and NGOs on which it is based contributed to increasing the cost-effectiveness of the programme. Indeed, the costs, cited in Figure 11, compare very favourably with the costs of existing outpatient services. Moreover, there are also cost savings to beneficiaries of the home care programme in Cambodia, in that the network provides consumer education in terms of which treatments are most cost-effective.[32]

Perhaps the key lesson related to costs from the case studies is the need to balance the expectations (both internal and external to the organization itself) of the scaling up with an understanding of available resources and costs. As mentioned above, NGOs often suffer from a lack of knowledge about both – from a lack of expertise necessary to measure both economic and financial costs, and from uncertainty over the available financial resources to support the scaling-up process. A recurrent theme in the case studies was the emergence of unexpected costs as the scaling up proceeded. In TASO's experience, for example, unanticipated costs were associated with the continued – and unplanned – need for supervision of 'TASO-like' services. In the case of ASI, the scaling-up process required much more technological equipment, specialized staff for evaluation and other purposes not envisioned in the original plan. Similarly, the International HIV/AIDS Alliance found that assistance to linking organizations in terms of both institutional and technical support consumed a much greater share of budgets than initially foreseen. Representatives of several organizations – such as PSG and the Cambodia Home Care Network Group – note that the irregular supplies of key commodities (such as condoms or treatments for STIs and home care treatments) limit the effectiveness of their programmes.

Despite the many difficulties outlined above in measuring the costs of scaling up, it is clear that the more knowledge NGOs are able to acquire about costs, the greater their relative bargaining position will be with the donor organizations on which most depend for funding. As Jeff O'Malley notes about the experience of the International HIV/AIDS Alliance: 'From the perspective of the Alliance's executive director, the Alliance's most significant mistake in its first two years was its failure to convene stakeholders to agree a new business plan and new targets in light of real commitments and restrictions rather than original projections and hopes.'

Clearly, more information is needed on the cost implications of scaling up NGO programmes. This is not to suggest that the effectiveness of scaling up should be measured on cost criterion alone, but that this is one critical piece of information that currently many NGOs, NGO support organizations and donors are uncertain about. One constraint in generating this information is the lack of understanding of economic definitions of cost benefit and cost effectiveness, and how to use these concepts in overall judgements. It is thus critical that NGO staff be familiar with, and not intimidated by, such concepts. Being able to apply costing analyses to one's own programmes would clarify NGOs' objectives in scaling up as well as their ability to measure whether they are achieving their declared objectives efficiently.

CHAPTER EIGHT

Challenges in scaling up HIV/AIDS efforts

RISKS AND CONCERNS ABOUT SCALING UP IN GENERAL

As the role of NGOs in social development has expanded over the past several decades, a number of criticisms have emerged. Among these are arguments that their impact would be greater if they looked self-critically at both their internal structures and processes, and their comparative advantage relative to government in particular. These criticisms are instructive in thinking about a process of scaling up which would expand the role of NGOs even further. Some have criticized NGOs for increasingly taking on tasks more appropriate to the state, although they have recognized that this has often been prompted by the prevailing context of structural adjustment and indebtedness in many countries. Ironically, NGOs themselves are often critical of these macro-economic policies yet find themselves increasingly pushed into the role of large-scale service providers, effectively substituting for the public sector (Edwards and Hulme 1992). Part of this may be attributed to the preference of donors to fund service provision that has concrete and visible outcomes, as opposed to less tangible advocacy efforts whose impact is difficult to measure. Yet not only does this shift have a major impact on the institutional culture of the NGO, but it can put them in a very different political role nationally, not to mention subverting the original aims of the organization.

In this context, the greatest concern has been expressed about what many have observed to be a prevailing tendency for NGOs to become more accountable to their external funders than to their declared constituency. In their book *NGOs, States and Donors: too close for comfort?*, Edwards and Hulme (1997) point to evidence that NGOs are 'losing their roots' as they increasingly serve the interests of donors, and to a lesser degree governments, rather than the poor and disempowered whom they set out to help. And scaling up might only exacerbate this tendency. Pearce voices a widely held view that: 'Without meaningful accountability to their "beneficiaries", scaling them up could seriously distance them from the poor and their own social structures' (Pearce 1993). Indeed, despite the claims of NGOs to represent the interests of their beneficiaries and respond to their needs, there are often few mechanisms to ensure that this is the case. For the most participatory-oriented organizations such needs make themselves felt precisely because the NGO faces the community daily, but as the scale at which NGOs operate increases, such close interaction, and consequently the scope for local participation, may be reduced.

Several authors have pointed to the fact that the increasingly influential relationship between donors and NGOs often creates processes whereby the structures and values of the NGO come to mirror those of the funding organization (Charlton 1995; Fowler 1991; Edwards and Hulme 1997). Moreover, complicated reporting procedures may stimulate the expansion of departments within the NGO to respond to such demands, thus increasing the bureaucratization of the organization. A premium may be placed on the employment of English-speaking graduates who are able to prepare polished proposals for donor consumption and this may distort the interaction with local communities, as well as the salary structure of the organization. White observes that increased size of NGOs serving the poor in Bangladesh has 'inevitably meant increased distance from the grassroots and the early pioneering vision has been replaced by an ethic of efficiency and professionalism' (White 1999: 321).

DONOR FUNDING

Many of the above critiques have also been levelled at NGOs active within HIV/AIDS. Although it is recognized that an increased level of donor support is necessary to increase the scale of operations, many have pointed to the damage created by a sudden influx of a large amount of donor funding.[33] If there has not been sufficient internal reflection regarding the strategic use of the funds – such as in a thoughtful process of preparing for scaling up – the influx of money is likely to diminish creative effort within the organization and may jeopardize the effectiveness of its programmes. Moreover, as organizations increasingly compete in chasing donor funds, this is likely to create jealousies and rivalries with other organizations that should be natural allies in efforts to increase the impact on HIV/AIDS.

Some have noted that receiving an increasing scale of funds – particularly if this is available through official channels negotiated with the state – may make NGOs less critical of government policy and inclined to shift away from an advocacy role (Sittitrai 1994). This has been observed in Australia, where the increasing official recognition of AIDS councils has prompted their expansion into large service-delivery organizations whose autonomy from the state is increasingly questioned.[34]

The risks associated with donor funding depend on the sources of such funds, and in many ways the nature of HIV/AIDS funding in the current era is dynamic. Two phenomena are particularly noteworthy, namely the increasing proportion of funding for NGOs coming from corporations and private foundations such as the Gates Foundation, and the creation in 2001 of the Global Fund Against AIDS, Tuberculosis and Malaria. Both of the trends imply that funding is likely to come in larger chunks of money, making some of the concerns about donor influence or agenda setting and NGO absorptive capacity all the greater.

With increased commitment for donor organizations to work on HIV/AIDS and to increase their budgetary allocations to it, particularly since the Durban conference and the creation of the Global Fund, there is growing competition among donors for NGOs to support. There is also concern that in the desire to spend these larger budgets, donors seek to commit larger amounts of money at one time to NGOs. There is a risk that donor funding may proceed at levels beyond the existing absorptive capacity of NGOs, and thus stifle their existing good efforts. To avoid such problems, clearly NGOs themselves need to refine tools for assessing their own capacity.[35] The ultimate risk is that the need of donor agencies to disburse larger amounts of money to local organizations may distort their original objectives or capacities. As Decosas, who has voiced this fear and is critical of the preoccupation of international organizations with scaling up, notes: 'A scaled up local response is no longer a local response, it becomes something else' (Decosas 2000: 16).

As noted in Chapter 5, closer associations between NGOs and the private sector – for example, by accepting corporate funding – bring both benefits and disadvantages. Some NGOs fear that greater reliance on funding from private sources may compromise their independence, restrict their ability to criticize or, in the worst case, implicate them in the marketing efforts of commercial enterprises. The advantages of greater access to ideas, information and influence may compensate for some of these disadvantages.

It is still too early to judge the likely impact of the Global Fund on NGOs' approaches to scaling up. Certainly the very existence of the Global Fund has already increased attention to HIV/AIDS, TB and malaria. It is estimated that funds available through the Global Fund – although not reaching the targets set – have already provided a 50% boost to the amount of financing available for the developing world to confront these diseases.[36] From the perspective of NGOs, the fact that NGOs are included on its governing board and technical review panel, and must be included in the application process at national level, is promising. Nevertheless, NGOs cannot apply directly except in situations where there is no functioning government. Thus it will depend on national governments as to whether NGOs will actually get a share of this money.

A less analysed feature of increased levels of donor support is how it may affect the local reputation of the organization and community perceptions of its activities. Hyden and Lanegran (1991), in a 'political mapping' of the AIDS epidemic in East Africa, argue that HIV/AIDS agenda setting within Africa has been overly dominated by international donors and Northern NGOs. Others within the HIV/AIDS sector, such as Decosas,[37] have argued that donor agencies have played too prominent a role in influencing HIV management in southern Africa. This reinforces the perception among Africans of AIDS as foreign and of outsider determination to prove that AIDS originated in Africa.

CULTURAL AND POLITICAL RESISTANCE

One of the greatest obstacles to HIV/AIDS prevention is the extent of stigma surrounding the disease, with its attendant association with 'illicit' or 'immoral' sex, fatal disease and death (Gilmore and Somerville 1994; Herek 1999). While cultural perceptions of the origin of the disease vary, such stigma has been identified across cultures (Goldin 1994).[38] Stigma itself creates resistance to people in the general population recognizing their own high personal levels of risk behaviour, since they feel the fact that they do not belong to a stigmatized 'high-risk group' makes them safe. It tends to motivate fear, which in turn prompts denial and failure to accept vulnerability or the reality of infection. This has been a main reason why political leaders have been reluctant in many developing and industrialized countries to accept and take responsibility for HIV.

Early messages in the North, which were based on fear and implied that anyone infected was careless or immoral ('if you behave yourself, you won't get HIV') or guilty ('it's all your own fault if you are infected') have contributed enormously to the stigma associated with HIV. These models inspired many of the messages developed in Southern campaigns. That is, they were based on Western, not local, cultural values and assumptions.

Given the sensitivity and stigma surrounding HIV/AIDS it is not amenable to the simpler strategies of scaling up, such as the process which Myers (1996) refers to as explosion (or implementing a large-scale intervention suddenly to achieve maximum coverage in a short time). 'Explosion' is more characteristic of, for example, immunization or literacy campaigns. While in some relatively non-controversial areas such as blood safety, 'explosion' may be possible as an approach in HIV/AIDS, in most aspects a slower pace and less visible nature of expansion may be more appropriate. Moreover, the stigma surrounding HIV/AIDS may make it difficult to mobilize sufficient demand for scaled-up services, rendering it particularly important to communicate the aims of the intervention as scaling up proceeds.

In some cases where stigma is particularly strong, NGOs have learned that it may be more appropriate to promote services for the general population, rather than making it explicit that it is for people with HIV/AIDS – such as, for example, expanding access to care for the chronically ill. Similarly, peer educators working in HIV/AIDS may prefer to be seen as community health educators because of the stigma associated with HIV/AIDS (Horizons 2000c).

While there are strong arguments for such an approach, there are also questions to be asked about whether disguising HIV/AIDS activities in anticipation of adverse reactions may actually perpetuate the stigma associated with HIV/AIDS. Some organizations have chosen, despite the attached stigma, to be completely transparent about their intentions. TASO staff, for example, always travel in vehicles explicitly marked TASO, whose reputation as an AIDS organization is known. At the same time, there may be risks regarding the difficulty of maintaining confidentiality and anonymity with such an approach.

As stated above, NGOs have clear advantages in dealing with stigmatized groups. Often they are able to do so because they operate on a small enough scale so as not to threaten or work against prevailing religious or cultural norms, and not at a large enough scale as to pose any political worries to government. Yet if they choose to expand their activities with such groups (strategy 1), they may perversely increase the latter's vulnerability to state repression or social prejudice. If their scaling-up strategy aims to catalyse other organizations (strategy 2) and they choose deliberately to work with government, they may well confront political and legal restrictions in working with these groups. In Egypt, for example, the National AIDS Programme cannot work with sex workers, since commercial sex work is illegal there. Similarly, in Pakistan, homosexuality is against the law.

At a political level, governments may be reluctant to draw national or international attention to HIV/AIDS because of the fear of tarnishing their national image or of a detrimental effect on crucial economic sectors such as tourism. Moreover, they may be averse to the kinds of alliance and networking among NGOs which scaling up necessitates. This depends on the degree to which the political climate is one that discourages or encourages the role of NGOs generally, and what legislation exists regarding oversight of their activities.

GREATER VISIBILITY

In many respects, increasing the scale of HIV/AIDS activities may bring greater visibility or prominence to specific organizations but perhaps more importantly to their constituencies. Depending on the political and social context in which NGOs operate, this may be beneficial or detrimental. In cases where it increases the stigma associated with HIV/AIDS or risks increasing discrimination against marginal social groups, such as sex workers or drug users, this visibility may have very negative effects. By contrast, in the case of some low-prevalence settings, such as Ecuador and the Philippines, this may be a necessary step to increase public awareness and give the groups involved greater negotiating power. It is, however, in low-prevalence countries that targeting marginalized groups with prevention interventions may be the most effective strategy to slow the spread of the virus. Thus scaling up efforts in these settings may mean considering increasing efforts in two very different directions: to stop the spread of the epidemic from particularly vulnerable populations on the one hand, and to change attitudes among the wider population on the other.

PROMOTING 'COMMUNITY PARTICIPATION'/ FACILITATING COMMUNITY RESPONSE

The foregoing discussion has argued for participatory processes during scaling up. These give beneficiaries a clear voice in defining directions and activities of HIV/AIDS organizations, and involve affected communities and individuals in the design of interventions. Yet, those who are members of the 'community' of interest in HIV/AIDS may well be diffuse, not organized along geographic or social lines, and may themselves resist efforts to promote their 'participation'. Asthana and Oostvogels (1996), in a cogent analysis of the obstacles to community participation in HIV prevention among female sex workers in Madras, India, found that sex workers there came from diverse social backgrounds, worked in a range of establishments and had varied access to support structures. Their ability to organize is therefore 'limited by the fact that they are locked into unequal power relationships with brothel-owners, madams and pimps and often too isolated and powerless to act individually or collectively' (Asthana and Oostvogels 1996: 133). Yet, in the end the women prefer to rely on such patrons – no matter how unequal the relationship – because it is a 'least risk strategy in extremely precarious circumstances' (Asthana and Oostvogels 1996: 146).

The objectives of the International HIV/AIDS Alliance (described in Case Study 11) in scaling up an approach to community action in HIV/AIDS is to encourage and provide the resources to communities to respond to HIV/AIDS rather than scaling up specific evidence-based HIV/AIDS interventions. Its approach is to strengthen both the institutional capacity and HIV/AIDS-related expertise of so-called 'linking organizations' in countries which in turn seek out and support local organizations to broaden the national response to the epidemic.

INCORPORATING DIVERSITY

Scaling up HIV/AIDS programmes beyond the borders of particular communities inevitably brings organizations into contact with a greater diversity of 'beneficiaries', whether in terms of social class or background, educational levels or income (Smith and Colvin 2000). Given how social attitudes about HIV/AIDS are often closely tied to such background variables,[39] developing messages and approaches that are suitable to this new diversity is challenging. Where initial

Case Study 11   The International HIV/AIDS
Alliance. Promoting local responses to HIV/AIDS from
an international level

The experience of the UK-based International HIV/AIDS Alliance in
scaling up its support for community action on HIV/AIDS internationally illustrates a scaling-up strategy premised on a commitment to community action by local NGOs and CBOs, rather than to expanding any
particular type of programme or intervention. Its approaches to doing
so, however, evolved considerably over time due to its own learning,
donor pressure and changing contexts for NGOs active in HIV/AIDS. In
seeking to have an international impact, the Alliance had to make critical choices as to which countries to focus on at what stage in the
scaling-up process – an experience which may have valuable lessons for
other organizations operating at the international level.

The Alliance was formally established in December 1993. The following quotation from the original proposal for support captures much
of the thinking that informed the Alliance's creation:

*Effective HIV/AIDS prevention, care and community support pro-
grammes require changes to individual attitudes and sexual behaviour
which can only be brought about by a sustained and massive mobil-
isation of communities which, whilst small individually, together add
up to a large-scale response.*

(Lenton 1993: 3–4).

The core mechanism of scaling up by the Alliance is identifying or establishing national mechanisms (later called 'linking organizations') and providing them with technical and financial support. These linking
organizations support NGOs already working on HIV/AIDS in their country to scale up, catalyse new groups to begin responding to AIDS, and
help both those new to HIV/AIDS and those already engaged in it
through providing organizational and technical support.

From the Alliance's inception it was anticipated that it would support
the expansion of other organizations in developing countries through
'organizational expansion' (strategy 1), as well as through 'mainstreaming in development' (strategy 5). After the first three years of its activities,
of the total of 220 organizations in seven countries that had received
financial and technical support for HIV/AIDS work, 200 were health or
development organizations rather than specifically HIV/AIDS groups.

The scaling-up strategy of the Alliance can be divided into distinct
chronological stages. During the first start-up period, from 1994 to

1996, it focused on community-level responses to prevention, care and (to very limited degree) alleviating the impact of HIV/AIDS, and national-level NGO/CBO support. In each of the 50 sites where the Alliance was active, a participatory community assessment was undertaken, leading to project design, increased community mobilization and improved community ownership. Following assessment, programme and project design included peer education programmes for young people and vulnerable groups, participatory prevention, community discussion groups and interactive awareness-raising activities. Self-help groups for people living with HIV/AIDS were also created and supported. National-level NGO/CBO support included assessments of national NGO/CBO sector strengths and weaknesses, the establishment and management of grant-making facilities, the development of a limited range of methodologies to identify and respond to NGO/CBO technical support needs, and partnership building and external relations for partner organizations.

After two years of operation, it was acknowledged that it was too early and too difficult to assess the impact of this work on the epidemic, but the Alliance's and other evaluations indicated that promising approaches were being promoted at a community level, as reflected in the following citation from an evaluation document:

When there is uncertainty about what contextual changes are appropriate or most significant, a valid strategy is to enable the people who are closest to the problem to decide, to experiment with different approaches, and to see what works. This is the methodological approach taken by the International HIV/AIDS Alliance, which offers one example of how to develop contextual interventions in HIV/AIDS prevention and care.

(USAID 1996).

Despite these overall positive assessments, the Alliance's external evaluation and other analyses pointed out some problems and controversies with the Alliance's approach and performance. These included, for example, concern that a greater proportion of expenditure than anticipated was absorbed in support and operational costs of linking organizations, and the view that it was unlikely that the Alliance itself could increase its operating budget significantly. There was strong pressure to pay more attention to quality and impact of interventions and responses, and a strong desire for the Alliance to play an increased role in sharing lessons learned and influencing others.

A new scale-up strategy was developed by the Alliance and endorsed by its donors in February 1997. It was based on the implicit assumption that, rather than being concerned about finding a global mechanism to deliver funds to community level, donors and multilateral agencies now had a growing appreciation of the Alliance's role in transferring lessons learned and influencing policy. Thus, moving from a catalytic strategy, the Alliance increasingly engaged in influencing policy (strategy 4).

During this period the Alliance actively discouraged investment in broad public awareness-raising programmes designed to serve the general public, and income-generation activities. In contrast, there was a growing awareness of the importance of concurrent community action to address supply of services and commodities for prevention and care and to stimulate demand for these services, while taking account of contextual factors contributing to the spread of HIV/AIDS including gender roles and stigma. More support was therefore channelled into following up discussion groups with outreach programmes, home care initiatives which integrated prevention and referrals, and the promotion of the involvement of people with HIV/AIDS. Gender issues such as violence against women and creating a sense of responsibility among men and boys, and sexually transmitted infection (STI) service delivery including condom promotion were all emphasized. Peer education and community development activities with marginalized communities key to the dynamics of the epidemic were encouraged. New pilot activities included harm reduction and prevention of sexual transmission with people who inject drugs, community mobilization linked to voluntary testing and counselling, and a response to the needs of orphans and vulnerable children. Links between care, prevention and impact alleviation began to be emphasized, and community-based advocacy took a higher priority.

By the end of 2000, the Alliance had worked with NGOs or CBOs from 25 countries, and was supporting ongoing NGO/CBO support programmes in 13 countries. The linking organizations had provided technical and financial support to over 1520 projects implemented by over 950 different NGOs and CBOs, about 85% of which were not AIDS groups. Many of the linking organizations also became key institutions influencing their national policy environments. Perhaps most notably, the Alliance's shift in strategy in 1997 allowed it to maintain (and even expand to some degree) the development and support of in-country NGO support systems, which in turn assist local NGOs and CBOs which organize and facilitate prevention, care and mitigating the impact of the epidemic.

The scaling-up process documented here illustrates a number of tensions that are likely to beset other similar efforts to scale up from an international base. First, the fact that the Alliance has an unusual structure of a 'two-tier umbrella programme' (meaning it acts as an international umbrella organization but supports in-country umbrella organization) has meant that tensions and synergies between local actors (implementing CBOs and NGOs) and national actors (linking organizations and their donors) are almost always mirrored between national actors (linking organizations) and international actors (the Alliance secretariat and its donors).

Second, from the start, the Alliance was committed to 'community-led' approaches to scaling up, as opposed to seeking to expand 'evidence-based' interventions in a 'top-down' fashion. However, through a combination of donor pressure and internal decisions, it began to promote more aggressively what it perceived as good practice. In its experience, the strongest and most sustainable initiatives are rooted in processes such as participatory community assessment and national-level decision-making about priorities and strategies, and are informed by 'expert' advice on matters such as key populations for epidemic dynamics and effective strategies. Balancing these perspectives and processes is slower and more intensive than either a straightforward replication of standard interventions or a laissez-faire approach of funding what the community wants to do.

Finally, there has been a clear tension for the Alliance between intensifying programmes in a smaller number of countries and having some involvement in more countries and regions. Initially, its choice of countries to work in reflected a strategy to test its approach in both low- and high-prevalence settings, and in countries with weaker and stronger NGO sectors, and also to establish a programme base in each of Africa, Asia and Latin America and to avoid particularly complex settings in the start-up period. Funding pressures have had more influence than programme strategy on these choices, however, as scaling up has proceeded.

Probably the costs per person reached would have been significantly lower had the Alliance worked in fewer countries and languages with the same level of overall funding. The politics and processes of organizational growth and fund-raising are central to any strategy to achieve more impact, and it is difficult to say whether the Alliance could have achieved more with a more focused strategy, or if its attempts to respond to perceived donor pressures and funding availability were essential to its survival and growth.

activities against HIV/AIDS began in primarily urban, middle-class movements, for example, efforts need to be made to transcend this narrow focus. This constraint would argue for a phased programme of implementation, rather than a sudden expansion or explosion, to give the organization time to adapt to and learn from the diverse settings and how best to work with constituencies from a wider range of socio-economic backgrounds.

THE PACE OF SCALING UP

The rapid spread of the HIV/AIDS epidemic calls for urgent measures to expand the scale of all activities to stem the progress of the epidemic. It is clear that the challenge for NGOs in HIV/AIDS is to find a balance between moving at an appropriate pace to mobilize demand and adapt the intervention to local social contexts and often highly stigmatized groups, at the same time generating enough momentum and sufficient political commitment to sustain the effort. The pace of expansion is not usually set by internal or micro-level concerns alone, but rather the overall context in which NGOs operate can be highly influential. For example, as argued above in the discussion of motivations, often the rapid spread of the epidemic, or economic and political factors, can play a key role in calling for a more rapid response in the face of growing need. On a positive note, where there is a surge in political commitment at the national level, or internationally, as was the case following the International Conference on AIDS in Durban in July 2000, for example, the pace of scaling up is likely to quicken. As will be discussed below, there are dangers that higher levels of international funding for HIV/AIDS may dictate the pace of expansion at a rate faster than the capacity of NGOs to sustain that activity.

RISK OF FAILURE

Perhaps the most poignant risk in scaling up HIV/AIDS programmes is that of failure, with disappointed expectations on the part of beneficiaries, NGO staff and funding institutions. As Avina notes, failed expansion has been the reason for the demise of many NGOs (Avina 1993: 466). Organizations considering scaling up need to bear this risk in mind when making their decisions: do they have the capacity to do scale up, the programmatic maturity and sufficient funding to sustain a greater scale of activity?

All NGOs face challenges and risks if they attempt to scale up their activities to have a greater impact. These difficulties are arguably even greater in the field of HIV/AIDS because of the stigma attached to the disease and the sensitivity of defining and acting upon risky behaviour. The challenges are not only programmatic; scaling up poses complex demands on institutions themselves and may result in substantial changes to their way of operating, their internal decision-making and their staffing needs. Some of these internal dimensions will be addressed in Chapter 9.

PART III

INSTITUTIONAL IMPLICATIONS

CHAPTER NINE

Internal dimensions of scaling up

PREPARING FOR SCALING UP

In most analyses of scaling-up processes, emphasis is placed on the external, programmatic dimensions, with much less attention paid to the internal, organizational questions which are perhaps equally important. Indeed, the reasons behind failure to scale up may lie more within a given NGO, in terms of inappropriate leadership, management or structures, than outside. Moreover, the little published literature there is on these concerns focuses on the experience of Northern, as opposed to Southern, NGOs (see, for example, Hodson 1992; Billis and MacKeith 1992).

This deficiency applies even more strongly to analysis of the internal implications of scaling up for NGOs active in HIV/AIDS. Very few organizations actually work with their staff or review their internal processes in preparation for the demands of scaling up. The experience of KANCO in Kenya is exceptional and instructive in this regard. Having made the shift from a voluntary to professional organization, and having established an office in 1993–94, it expanded rapidly and was successful in obtaining a higher level of funds. At this point, the NGO began to see some of its bigger programmes collapse, and went through a period of institutional reflection to analyse what was happening within the institution. It developed a questionnaire for staff concerning the goals of the organization, its achievements and what people most enjoyed about working for the organization. This process informed a thorough strategic plan that laid the basis for a reorganization. Among the new procedures introduced were job analysis and evaluation, new financial and personnel procedures, a staff appraisal system and more attention to sustainability (see Case Study 12).

Planning and preparing for scaling up could be made easier by viewing the process as a project in itself. Having a clear plan with objectives, indicators to measure success at achieving these objectives, and planned activities to achieve transition to a different scale of operation

Case Study 12   The Kenya AIDS NGO
Consortium. Internal change for greater programmatic effectiveness

The Kenya AIDS NGO Consortium (KANCO) was founded in 1990 by a group of seven health and development NGOs that had added an HIV/AIDS component to their existing programmes. It has since grown to coalition of some 600 NGOs/CBOs and religious organizations dealing with HIV/AIDS/STI activities in Kenya and is a main reference point for NGOs working on HIV/AIDS in the country.

The transition from an initially small voluntary organization to a large-scale national professional operation has been rapid, and as the expansion proceeded KANCO staff had the foresight to perceive the need for a substantial period of institutional reflection to plan further expansion.

The main goal of the consortium is to improve the response to the epidemic by fostering networks among NGOs and between NGOs and the government, and by increasing the capacity of NGOs to work on HIV/AIDS. Such networking is facilitated by providing fora to share resources and enhance collaborative efforts. KANCO also runs a clearing house of information on HIV/AIDS information, education and communication materials to provide broad access to organizations interested in HIV/AIDS. The centre receives a monthly average of 350 enquiries.

Unlike many of the case study organizations presented in this book, KANCO's scaling-up process was explicitly aimed at achieving a national scope of activities, and it simultaneously acts at the central level as well as through district-level networks. It has endeavoured to do so by working through, and strengthening, existing capacity within its member organizations rather than establishing field offices of its own. An explicit part of KANCO's mandate, for example, is to assist member organizations in strategic planning, organizational development and financial accounting.

Having made the shift from a voluntary to a professional organization, and having established an office in 1993–94, KANCO expanded rapidly and received a higher level of funds. However, its staff began to see some of the bigger programmes collapse, and therefore went through a period of institutional reflection to analyse what was happening within the institution.

In 1997, KANCO identified the need to expand and strengthen its services, enhance its visibility and increase its capacity. With the assistance of consultants in organizational development, it developed an implementation plan to assist in designing a strategy to support its member organizations and their constituencies more effectively, particularly at district level.

Organizational development was thus used as a tool which helped KANCO to identify constraints or 'crisis points' in its structure to inform the organization whether it needed to operate in different ways to improve its effectiveness. Individual employees were interviewed, including the director and all staff working in administration, policy and advocacy, to explore why they chose to work at KANCO, whether their own personal objectives were achieved there and how staff perceive KANCO objectives. The surveys were then followed by a diagnostic workshop attended by staff, board members and volunteers that focused on analysing and summarizing the results of the staff surveys.

The next steps of the process of institutional reflection consisted of a participatory development of a five-year strategic plan, which concentrated on a limited set of key questions. A main objective of the exercise was to make discussion of KANCO's mission and organizational vision explicit in order to foster a staff consensus that would prove critical as a base for future expansion. This planning process introduced participants to the importance of medium- and long-term planning for the organization, but at the same time allowed participants to express their own expectations and fears. It also included an explicit analysis of KANCO stakeholders and the external environment that would support or hinder the scaling-up process. The outcomes of the process were the articulation of three key goals, including developing a competent central secretariat, strengthening district networks and enhancing advocacy capacity for members to respond to HIV/AIDS policy issues effectively.

In short, KANCO staff felt that the internal process of reflection, while ambitious and time-consuming, increased the transparency with which the organization operated, increased staff morale and staff ownership over the organization's mission, and ultimately created a more solid base for the organization's external programme of goals of responding to HIV/AIDS in Kenya.

would help to ensure that scaling up is not haphazard. It would also strengthen the perception of scaling up as a more achievable and straightforward process, rather than as something very different from an NGO's normal programming.[40] Partly because NGOs do not usually see scaling up in the same way that they view the implementation of a project, there is little experience of developing indicators and the means of measuring progress while scaling up. Such planning and monitoring would make scaling up less daunting and more manageable. Nevertheless there are circumstances in which scaling up is in response to a recognition of a new opportunities, needs or even threats which demand urgent action.

Whether an organization has the time to reflect on internal and external prerequisites for scaling up both before and during implementation partly depends on the nature of its funding. If the entire scaling-up process is financed from a single donor, often its pace may be dictated by that particular donor's demands. PSG in Zimbabwe has a policy of maintaining funding from five diverse donors, partly in order to ensure the requisite programme and institutional autonomy.

CHANGES IN INSTITUTIONAL CULTURE AND PROCESSES

Institutional culture and structures are inevitably affected as organizations expand the scale of their activities. Changing roles of staff and board in the process of scaling up can be very threatening, and may lead to loss of staff. Decisions formerly made on the basis of trust and informality may give way to more formal structures and increased hierarchy (Hodson 1992), and involve different people. How managers help the staff of their organizations to weather these dramatic changes is critical to the success of the scaling up. Staff may be used to a process of ownership and participation that is possible in a smaller organization but may not be sustained as scaling up proceeds (Billis and MacKeith 1992). Expansion may also require an increased functional specialization between parts of the organization, increased capacity to raise resources and standardized delivery mechanisms to reduce unit costs (Edwards and Hulme 1992, 1996). Increased emphasis on professionalism and efficiency may come to replace the 'value consensus' and mission goals that motivated the establishment of the NGO in the first place (Hodson 1992).

These processes may be particularly true of organizations addressing HIV/AIDS where the staff's personal commitment to the aims and particular approaches to HIV/AIDS, which they feel are rare, may inspire a particularly strong sense of staff ownership and thus resistance to change. The greater diversity within the organization and the increased proportion of professional staff, as opposed to volunteers, as organizations expand into service-delivery organizations, for example, can sometimes limit the ability to work with affected communities.[41] Both these trends may jeopardize the former commitment of the organization to providing labour-intensive, personalized care.

SIAAP, in India, found that the professionalization accompanying scaling up can bring tensions. Its staff found it difficult to prevent agenda setting by professional consultants, whether Indian or Western. The expanding role of a high-profile professional intervention with such assistance created some friction within the institution, particularly when compared to the efforts in community outreach and advocacy. These trends may again reduce the close relationship between community and organization which is often essential for effective work on HIV/AIDS

When, as is often the case, only certain programmes of an organization are scaled up, there may be a sense of resentment and competition over resources from staff of other programmes. This was true of the experience of both SIAAP and Naz, for example. In the former case, the counselling programme expanded much more rapidly than the other programmes, and in the latter, the Healthy Highways initiative began to command a greater amount of resources and attention, creating internal tensions. Similarly, staff at ASI found that the most difficult challenge of the scaling-up process was the need to balance the limited funds and resources between existing programmes and projects. Although the organization did compose a strategic plan to guide the expansion with the assistance of an external consultant, the resource demands of the expansion were greater than expected. The need for more equipment, specialized staff for evaluation and other staff were not anticipated in the original plan. As a result, staff members at times felt that resources were being diverted from existing programmes. Directors held several sessions with the entire staff to keep them informed about the direction of the scaling-up process.

INVOLVING VOLUNTEERS

Many of the organizations that expanded their HIV/AIDS activities did so through the explicit recruitment or increased involvement of volunteers. For example, AMSED in Morocco saw this as a key strategy for reaching more people. Since volunteers usually come from the communities with which NGOs are working, are aware of existing services and often know the community members well, the clear benefit is the increased sense of community ownership over the project the involvement of volunteers brings. This was also the case for ASI, where volunteers with HIV/AIDS contributed both time and materials towards the building of a new clinic – a step that ASI sees as critical to the legitimacy of the effort. Similarly, the founder of PSG in Zimbabwe describes its programmes as almost entirely based on volunteers: 'Both prevention and mitigation share a common approach. They both work with community volunteers to deliver large-scale, economical, locally relevant services that increase community response capacity (see Case Study 1). And in Cambodia, volunteers in the Home Care programme are 'well placed to facilitate links with other community activities, to ensure access and accessibility of Home Care Teams, and are a major source of referral of new patients to the Home Care Teams' (Wilkinson et al. 2000: 57).

Often volunteers work as peer educators, who have been shown to be highly effective in a variety of settings in terms of fostering behavioural change, and also in generating demand for HIV-related services such as voluntary counselling and HIV testing and management of sexually transmitted infections (Horizons 2000c).

While the involvement of volunteers is likely to be an integral component of NGO scaling-up strategies, the contribution of volunteers may need to be formalized as the scaling up proceeds. ASI in Guatemala found that a critical step that improved their effectiveness was the recruitment of a manager to whom the volunteers report. The formalization of the contributions of volunteers or donated commodities will mean that the costs associated with scaling up may be significantly different to (and substantially larger than) the costs of running projects at current scales of activity. The costs, for example, of peer education programmes are often much higher than expected, given the need for training, support, supervision and to provide them with resource material and compensation (Horizons 2000c).

In a number of NGOs working on HIV/AIDS, volunteers play a key role in collecting data useful for monitoring projects. The same organizations have also noted the problem of quality entailed in relying solely on volunteers to collect data. Furthermore, the frequently high turnover of volunteers can be detrimental to institutional learning.

People living with HIV have a key part to play in the response to HIV, and while NGOs fully recognize this, they can be limited in the ways in which they implement such involvement. Volunteers who are HIV-positive are often highly motivated to help others, and their own needs can be overlooked, leading to both high turnover and burnout. Psychological support, payment of expenses and help with access to treatment are all essential to enable people with HIV to offer the involvement that makes a difference to the quality of programmes. Expansion means not only initial investment in recruitment and training of volunteers, but also planning for continuing support and training.

LEADERSHIP

Many innovative NGO efforts are led by charismatic, visionary leaders who pay relatively little attention to the establishment of participatory internal structures of governance (Fowler 1991; Edwards and Hulme 1992) and this has also been true of those active in HIV/AIDS (Sittitrai 1994). Yet the demands on leadership necessarily change as the organization enlarges its scale of activity. The question is then raised as to whether the leader who pioneered the scaling-up process is also the right person to lead the organization through the next stage.

In order to sustain expansion, it is imperative to reach consensus among staff about the objectives and approaches to scaling up. Moreover, in order to scale up operations, managers increasingly have to delegate to staff at lower levels or to leaders within the beneficiary community. Are they willing to give a prominent role to subordinate staff members and, for example, sex workers, in directing activities, and will due credit be given to them? And is attention being paid to the need to develop a second generation of leadership given that the scaling-up process is likely to take a long time? The leadership of any organization undertaking scaling up is likely to feel tension between the often conflicting processes of achieving efficiency for operating at a larger scale, encouraging participatory processes within the beneficiary community, and sustaining employee aspirations and motivations as the organization undergoes change (Hodson 1992).

CAPACITY

Capacity encompasses the number of people an organization can call on, the skills and experience these people have, and the systems, technical back-up and resources at an organisation's disposal. The process of scaling up revealed to SIAAP that while it had considerable technical skills, its organizational and administrative capacities were often inadequate to the task of coordinating the diverse activities that were being undertaken. As SIAAP describes it: 'There was no start-up period, no pre-planning and few people available to take responsibilities for the details of what was becoming a huge and complex enterprise that had to provide counselling, training and services.'

Thus scaling up may necessitate the hiring of new categories of staff or enlisting new board members with diverse skills, or the retraining of existing personnel, all of which may be very costly. As already described, it may also involve discovering new ways of working together, which can lead to the need to establish new sections. This may entail bringing in professional human resource staff for the first time and changing the way the organization copes with staff relations, or, as ASI's experience indicates, setting up new monitoring and evaluation capacity. With limited resources, expenditure and concentration on internal needs can be perceived as being in conflict with programming and meeting the needs of beneficiaries – a situation that calls for leadership and good communication within the organization.

In the case of KANCO in Kenya (see Case Study 12), the organization conducted a thorough strategic planning process. Operational outcomes of this exercise included a job analysis and evaluation, which led to the development of a grade-level system based on evaluation results; a salary survey which provided the basis for recommending a salary structure and prompted the creation of a staff pension and medical scheme; the creation of financial and personnel policy manuals; a staff appraisal system; and more attention being given to staff training to strengthen KANCO's ability to respond to donor requirements for financial management, analysis and reporting. A series of joint donors' meetings were then convened to explain KANCO's activities, constraints and future plans to the organization's main funders.

One key area that needs to be addressed is the avoidance of high staff turnover, given the need for institutional continuity during what is often a time-consuming scaling-up process. This may be a particular problem for organizations that have relied on volunteers, or where salary levels are not sufficient to keep talented staff. While NGOs in most fields face difficulties in maintaining continuity and retaining skilled and experienced staff, those in HIV/AIDS face particular constraints since 'the epidemic is so close to the people who are working in the epidemic' (Loughran 1995: 6). At the same time, NGOs working in HIV also recognize the value (though they often find it difficult to act on this) of including people with HIV both as staff members and as volunteers. This has been the experience, for example, of the Cambodia Home Care Programme where a number of key staff have died of HIV/AIDS. When an NGO loses key staff it may take a long time for the programme to regain momentum. This is a particular concern where programmes are working through volunteers to provide home care or community support, as people volunteering to support those with HIV are often motivated by their own direct experience of the epidemic, and are therefore more likely to be living with HIV themselves.

NGOs working on HIV/AIDS activities are beginning to face the dilemmas focused on the provision of treatment, in particular antiretrovirals, for staff and volunteers. Where there is no other access to such treatment, NGOs will have to make difficult decisions about whether to meet the costs themselves, and where to draw the line about who gets treatment and who does not. Such decisions include whether NGOs should provide drugs for employed staff if they cannot afford to do so for volunteers and beneficiaries.

There is also a need to build the capacity of staff to maintain good working relations with the organizations with which they will come into contact in the scaling-up process, whether other NGOs or governmental bodies. As the scaling up proceeds, such contact may be with an increasingly diverse range of organizations. Staff will need to document the processes and obstacles to scaling up and be able to communicate these lessons more broadly to stakeholders.

Once agreement has been reached on the objectives of scaling up, careful attention needs to be paid to creating appropriate incentives for staff – or personnel of the organizations one is trying to influence – to meet them. This is a particularly challenging task in sensitive areas such as HIV/AIDS, where the associated stigma creates a need to instil changes in attitude and approach.[42] An example of the difficulty of inspiring such attitudinal change is provided by the case of reproductive health in India. Following the International Conference on Population and Development (Cairo, 1994) the Indian government undertook a strong commitment to shifting the orientation of their population programmes from a vertical orientation to family planning to the wider and more comprehensive concept of reproductive health. Yet one of the main constraints to implementing this strategy is the difficulty of changing the approach of family planning cadres. The latter have been entrenched in ways of working that stress the goal of increasing contraceptive prevalence rates, as opposed to a more process-oriented approach of eliciting and addressing often sensitive reproductive health problems (Health Watch 1998).

If it is well planned and well managed, the process of expansion – although it may require change in attitude and ways of working – can in itself be a morale boost for staff, in conferring a sense of greater visibility, prominence and effectiveness. This positive outcome has been cited by a number of NGOs, including the PSG, ASI and KANCO.

RESOURCES AND MAKING SURE THEY ARE SUFFICIENT

Increasing the scale of activities – even if it is through partnerships with other organizations – will nearly always mean that there is a need for increased resources. This is another aspect of the dilemma NGOs face in allocating scarce resources, especially in the context of scaling up. If an organization is responding to an external need voiced by the people it is serving, it may seem controversial to spend more money on fund-raising, including the hiring of professional staff. On the other hand, expansion is unlikely to be successful without increased resources, and even if scaling up is in response to a push from one or more donors, these donors will themselves need to be supplied with reports and responses to demands. Also, as illustrated by ASI, many donors are better than one, which also means increased fund-raising and donor-relation capacity.

Examples abound of where NGOs feel that inadequate resources have been the single greatest constraint on their plans for scaling up. For example, ASI found that while there was strong national support for the programme, and it even received a number of donations from community members, funds were not always forthcoming in a steady stream that would finance a smooth expansion of the services being offered. Local donations did enable ASI to open a new and larger clinic, but there was no money to hire additional staff to handle the increased number of patients until much later. During this period, the staff were overworked and stressed.

Dutch government funding was critical in that it offered funding for the first three years of the expansion to support core staff in the time of strategic planning and allowed ASI to search for sources of long-term and sustainable revenue. The fact that no funding was available to fund the scaling-up process *per se* made it difficult to finance a formal evaluation of it, although informal internal reviews were conducted twice a year to evaluate the progress.

Scaling up itself may lead to a higher profile for the organization, and the need to be able to respond to interest from donors and possible funding opportunities arising from this may also become a key factor at a later stage.

Developing a fund-raising capacity could also lead to resentment among other sections of an organization, especially if there appears to be a diversion of funds from programmes. There could be implications for leadership, as it can be easy for a leader to become diverted into donor relations and fund-raising, leaving the rest of the scaling-up process adrift. High-profile or large-scale funding initiatives can also cause disruption by diverting time and attention – and therefore resources – into applications for new sources of funding.

There are positive examples of where a thoughtful fund-raising strategy has facilitated the scaling up of an NGO programme. Key to the success of PSG's scaling up has been its financial strategy and careful attention to measuring the costs of interventions and to keeping unit costs low. Administrative costs are also kept low (see Chapter 6) and PSG passes on 90 to 92.5% of all resources it receives in direct grants. Scaling up has been carefully planned in relation to available resources, with phased country-by-country expansion. PSG sought funding from donors who take a long-term perspective and are willing to work regionally. In general, donors tend to agree with the organization's time frame for scaling up because they are familiar with its budgets. To maximize the institution's autonomy, PSG has a deliberate strategy of diversifying its funding base, maintaining at least five sources of funding in each programme. The latter include support from multilateral/bilateral development agencies and private foundations, as well as private sector 'in kind' or 'in cash' donations (particularly in South Africa), community contributions and governmental subsidies, including personnel, grants and medical supplies and services.

DOCUMENTATION AND EVALUATION

Often overlooked in the haste to expand the scale of activities is the importance of building capacity to collect data, as well as to document the experience of scaling up or the indicators used to evaluate it. Greater attention to documentation of the process of scaling up is not only important as a motivating factor for staff, but also provides the opportunity to share success with others, thereby widening perception of need, widening constituencies involved and even stimulating new action

To be meaningful, the data collected must inform the scaling-up process and not be collected for its own sake. As noted above, PSG in Zimbabwe is exemplary in analysing the impact of each intervention in terms of behavioural change and cost to draw lessons for application elsewhere. And ASI uses volunteers to collect data that have – as shown above – identified dips in quality and prompted a revision of strategy. Much more can be done in general by NGOs to collect routine information on their activities and their impact to inform assessment of effectiveness.[43]

In some cases, even where there is desire to collect such information, it is not available because the programme approach is so new. Geoff Foster (see Case Study 10), describing the experience of establishing a community support programme for children affected by AIDS in Zimbabwe, noted that when it began, there were no known models of community support to children affected by AIDS. Therefore staff had no information on which to set targets for coverage, impact and sustainability. Similarly, Margarita Quevedo observed that most of the organizations KIMIRINA supports in Ecuador tend to lack access to data, and are weak in documenting their own programmes or conducting evaluations, and therefore scaling up tends to be a trial-and-error process.

It is evident that much more effort and time could be invested by NGOs themselves in developing criteria for assessing their own programmes. In evaluating the effects of scaling up, it is important that one relies on a range of indicators to give a fuller picture of change. Since reported sexual behaviour change is subject to bias, use of other criteria of change may be necessary. For example, the Family Health Trust's initiative in supporting Anti-AIDS Clubs in Zambia has found that there was no change in reported sexual behaviour among club members. There has, however, been an increase in young people reporting to health centres for screening and treatment of STDs (see Case Study 3).

Increasing the capacity of partner institutions to collect data and evaluate their effectiveness can be an objective of a scaling-up exercise. For example, the aims behind the establishment of FOCUS were not only to provide care to orphans in need, but also to provide data about numbers of orphans and vulnerable children, and to set up a community-based monitoring system that could identify emerging problems related to the care and support of orphaned children. Such a system would, for example, identify those orphans at risk of morbidity or malnutrition, or of educational or other forms of social deprivation (Foster et al. 1996).

Soliciting the views of beneficiaries in the evaluation of scale up is essential. For example, the FACT/FOCUS programme found that the initial efforts of communities to respond to the problem of orphans were successful in that: 'Community-based organizations were able to identify a high proportion of orphans living in their area, target those most in need, and provide regular visits and material support.' But when the orphans were asked for their views, they stated that they had understood that their guardians, rather than themselves, were being visited and assisted through the programme.

For organizations working in the field of HIV/AIDS now, the urgent need for scaling up to address the ever-increasing scale of the epidemic, and prevent or alleviate the human distress and grief which comes in its wake, may override the need for careful assessment and planning. If new initiatives in funding, such as the Global Fund for HIV/AIDS, TB and Malaria, stimulate an overall increase in funds available, and if other donors such as corporations and bilateral donors continue to wake up to the impact HIV is having on development, donor pressure as well as the demands of the epidemic itself will increase. In such circumstances, NGOs do not have the option of not responding. But there is also an obligation on the part of both donors and NGOs to learn from others' experience so that scaling-up efforts are as effective and constructive as possible, and so that expansion does not undermine the organization and become counter-productive.

CHAPTER TEN

Implications for donors and NGO support organizations in HIV/AIDS

The foregoing discussion suggests that it is not only those organizations that are interested in scaling up that need to reconsider the implications for their operations and internal management structures. Donors and AIDS-support organizations also need to adapt to be able to support the complex demands that the process of scaling up places on the institutions they support. This will not only entail changes in funding arrangements, but will also mean that staff of such organizations need a greater and more sophisticated understanding of what scaling up means beyond merely doing more or reaching more people. In particular, it calls for comprehension of the comparative advantage of NGOs individually and collectively in the context of the complex and evolving relationships between NGOs, governments and other players responding to the HIV/AIDS epidemic. It would also require having tailored strategies for working with NGOs trying to scale up their activities in different countries with different social, political and economic contexts and depending on the level of the epidemic among other factors.

LEVELS OF FUNDING AND TIMESCALE OF SUPPORT

The level of funding needed to enable a process of scaling up to occur is perhaps the most obvious prerequisite to facilitating, rather than undermining, NGOs' efforts. Yet few donors are willing to sustain commitment to an organization as they undergo the 'trial-and-error' process of expanding their operations, and these challenges are arguably more arduous in the field of HIV/AIDS. Indeed, the proliferation of highly visible pilot or 'boutique' projects, that UNAIDS (June 2000) among others criticizes, is at least partly due to the lack of available funding to replicate these on a larger scale. But equally important is the timescale of support, if one considers the time needed to prepare for scaling up, including conceiving and communicating ideas, encouraging participation of beneficiaries, adapting to diverse contexts and preparing the organization for change. Given the time demands and major institutional change scaling up requires, there is a need for donors to shift from short-term project finance to more long-term institutional support. This view is endorsed by a World Bank report on HIV/AIDS in Africa which states that: 'Sporadic or isolated activities are ineffective unless they are evaluated as pilot activities and revised and expanded based on what has been learned. To maximise their impact, programmes should be implemented for long periods based on need rather than on funding cycles' (World Bank 1999: 24).

To allocate sufficient budgets to NGOs for a meaningful and effective scaling up of their impact requires an understanding of approaches to costing NGOs' programmes. As noted in Chapter 7, there is a dearth of costing analysis of NGOs, and the few examples that do exist are mainly for governmental programmes. There tends to be a rather superficial assumption among many donor organizations active in HIV/AIDS that increasing the scale of activities necessarily implies greater economies of scale. As illustrated in Chapter 7, this may be true in the short term as programmes expand to reach more people. But over the long term, as greater investment in capacity is needed (which is very likely), or as NGOs move from relying on in-kind contributions to a larger scale of operations, or through formalizing the role of community volunteers to full employees, there may actually be diseconomies of scale. Finally, as Chapter 7 also illustrated with reference to the few case studies in this book which addressed the costs of scaling up, similar interventions are likely to be associated with very different costs across countries and even within the same country due to different levels of infrastructure and varying costs of inputs such as labour. Moreover, all costs may change rapidly over time in countries that have high inflation or which are undergoing economic upheaval associated with structural adjustment programmes. Devaluation – a critical recommendation of most structural adjustment programmes – for example, is likely to alter cost structures almost overnight. Thus, while further costing information on NGOs' efforts to scale up their activities is necessary and welcome, such data should be used judiciously.

BUILDING ABSORPTIVE CAPACITY

In a general discussion of the implications for donors of scaling up not specific to HIV/AIDS, Uvin refers to the simultaneous need to 'scale up the grassroots and scale down the summit' (by which he means international organizations). That is, they should 'adopt structures and modes of operation that allow local communities and NGOs to build their conceptual, operational and institutional capacities' (Uvin 1995: 506). This suggests the importance of providing sufficient resources and time to encourage reflection and learning, even when these do not necessarily translate into short-term, demonstrable outputs. Funding for expansion should take into consideration not only the external programme context but also the institutional prerequisites to scaling up, and the kind of intensive internal work required, such as conducted by KANCO, for example. Donor organizations also need to be self-critical and evaluate whether the onerous reporting requirements they impose on NGOs, for example, are always necessary or could be streamlined.

In many cases, the nature of donor funding complicates and undermines the scaling-up process of NGOs, and attention needs to be paid to avoiding such situations in the context of an overall increase in the level of funding for HIV/AIDS that we are now witnessing. For example, donors may contribute to the lack of planning for scaling up by making a sudden rash of funds available that has to be spent in a finite period. As the director of ASI put it: funders caused 'chaos' with the rapid pace of expansion they imposed on that organization. The experience of ASI illustrates that donors – at least in this case – did not envision the scaling-up process as such, leading to a 'feast and famine' financial situation at ASI. As staff at ASI put it: 'There were periods of rapid growth and periods of no growth due to erratic funding. . . A more comprehensive evaluation of the scaling-up process was difficult because no funding was available for the process itself. This made it difficult to assess the overall progress at the early stages.'

As noted in Chapter 9, a sensible strategy for NGOs is to have a policy of diversifying funding sources, so that their own autonomy is maximised. This does pose the risk of having different donors impose competing objectives on programming – with further implications for the balance between programmes within the organization. While such competing pressures and messages can have negative results, if they are managed well, they may ultimately benefit the organization.

For example, the International HIV/AIDS Alliance found that some of its donors were eager to see the organization expand its actual coverage of numbers of people, while some felt the quality of activities at local level was most important and others were encouraging the Alliance to take a more 'hands-off' influencing or advocacy role. In the end, the net result of these pressures was that the organization sought a healthy balance between intensive prevention and care work among populations key to epidemic dynamics, with broader awareness activities in the general population, as well as partnerships with governments to reach larger numbers of people vulnerable to HIV/AIDS.

It is critically important that both donors and NGO support organizations active in HIV/AIDS recognize the need for building institutional capacity as a goal in its own right, and not just as a 'delivery cost' for expanding the scale of particular interventions. The experience documented in this book of national NGOs, such as KIMIRINA, KANCO, PSG and the International HIV/AIDS Alliance among others, which have adopted a 'catalyst strategy' (strategy 2) to scaling up their impact, is indicative. They have recognized explicitly that their support to local development of HIV/AIDS-related organizations must be in more than technical aspects of HIV/AIDS and must also focus on NGO capacity-building. Investment in skills and capacity such as fund-raising, documentation, evaluation, policy analysis and advocacy, epidemiological surveillance and provision of training materials are all likely to have clear impact both on the organization itself and its effectiveness programmatically.

Similarly, both donors and AIDS support organizations need to address explicitly the capacity of NGOs to evaluate their own scaling-up efforts. This would encourage them to develop, for example, indicators which can be subject to scrutiny and which are acceptable to the funding organization but are not merely imposed and therefore often not appropriate. For example, the frequently used indicator of 'numbers of people reached' could be problematic, as the International HIV/AIDS Alliance discovered when one of its main funders required this criterion to evaluate all programmes funded by it. Not only was this indicator at odds with the organization's newly defined strategy for scaling up, which reflected a move from a catalytic strategy (strategy 2) to a more advocacy/influencing policy role (strategy 4) (see Case Study 11), but it could be interpreted in a variety of ways – people reached with services financed by the

Alliance; people reached by organizations influenced by the Alliance; people reached effectively or people reached at all.

AVOIDING THE 'ONE-SIZE-FITS-ALL' APPROACH

Implicit in having a greater understanding of what scaling up NGO programmes implies, is a recognition of the need to tailor – not only NGO, but also donor and NGO support organizations' scaling-up strategies – to varying contexts. That is, for example, how should a strategy for scaling up differ in a low- versus high-prevalence setting or according to different types of interventions? And, given how context-specific the social dynamics of the epidemic are, how are the proposed interventions tailored to social and cultural context in which the scaling up will proceed? These questions are now beginning to receive greater attention, but there is by no means international consensus on their answers. Those concerned with scaling up might reflect on how differences in approaches to scaling up may be applied at three levels:

- to different programmes within the same organization
- to different organizations within the same country
- between different countries (for those which work internationally).

Within individual organizations it is conceivable that certain activities are more amenable than others to scaling up or require different time frames for scaling up. Instead of concentrating all its resources and staff time on scaling up all interventions, an organization could, for example, scale up a particular intervention while leaving time, energy and creativity to experiment at a pilot level with other activities. Thus, while there are synergies to be gained in scaling up several HIV/AIDS programmes together (UNAIDS 2000a), which may also yield greater economies of scope, these may be better gained through complementarities among organizations rather than single organizations scaling up several demanding activities simultaneously.

That said, there are risks that donors may also fragment organizations' integrity by only emphasizing scaling up of individual strategies or interventions and not recognizing the synergies between them. Chapter 9 provided examples of NGOs such as ASI, SIAAP and the Naz Foundation where an increase in donor funding for particular programmes has created tension within organizations, as they are privileged over others and may usurp resources. This suggests that more flexible funding that allows organizations to allocate resources across interventions would be most effective, although for a number of reasons it may not be realistic.

Identifying and building on the appropriate balance between interventions may take a 'trial-and-error' period of learning. As the founder of SIAAP (see Case Study 5) aptly described: 'It took SIAAP four years of sustained community-based interventions with women in prostitution, truckers, blind people and people with HIV/AIDS to understand the need to include community organization, counselling and care as critical processes, perhaps even the first ones in any community-based intervention that aimed at empowerment as a fundamental outcome.' She drew a broader lesson of the importance of not singling out individual interventions for scaling up, without seeing the synergies between them. She illustrated her vision of these synergies and the importance of community organization (see Figure 12).

As elaborated on in the preceding chapters, in particular national contexts the pressure to scale up should not be applied

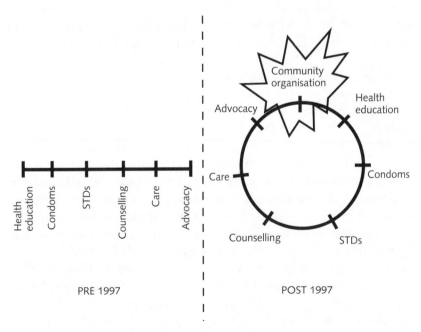

Figure 12   A vision of the shift from linear to integrated programming
Source: Presentation by Shyamala Nataraj of SIAAP at the Horizons/Alliance Seminar 2000.

indiscriminately across the board, no matter how high the level of the epidemic. Donors and NGO support organizations should not necessarily focus on selecting the most professional organizations for support, but should recognize that a range of types and sizes of organisation are complementary to one another and thus a portfolio of different types of investment at varying levels may be more effective.[44] This implies that it is critical for donors and AIDS support organizations to inform themselves of the comparative advantages of different types of institutional response to HIV/AIDS within a given country and how these relate to one another. There is the very real risk, for example, that donors searching for reputable and effective organizations to fund may swamp the successful models with unrealistic expectations. In Cambodia, for example, the very success of the fledgling Home Care Programme developed through a government–NGO collaboration is creating the risk of unrealistic expectations to have the home care teams also deal with malnutrition, tuberculosis and reproductive health.

As mentioned earlier, not all organizations or aspects of programmes are amenable to scaling up. Pressure to scale up – particularly if applied to community-based organizations whose very strength lies in their small-scale, local responses – may undermine the aspects of that institution's work which make it most effective in addressing the behavioural and social context of HIV/AIDS. As Decosas (2000: 16) has said: 'A scaled up local response is no longer a local response.'

Foster has articulated a powerful critique of the way in which donors, and indeed other external agencies, may ignore existing community initiatives to address HIV/AIDS and even – unknowingly or not – undermine them. The risk of such a trend is, if anything, greater with the increased influx of resources devoted to HIV/AIDS and the 'pipeline' problems of needing to spend a greater level of resources within a finite period of time. Foster is highly critical, for example, of the prevailing tendency among many donor organizations to pay community members for their involvement in HIV/AIDS. Foster and colleagues deliberately avoided such an approach in developing the FACT/FOCUS programme in Zimbabwe (see Case Study 10) supporting existing responses of community-based organizations. As Foster describes the relationship between FACT/FOCUS and the local community-based organizations involved: 'FACT did not employ or pay allowances to community members taking part in the programme, nor did it provide support directly to orphans – these might have undermined existing extended family care and led to dependency by community members. Instead, the co-ordinator identified a community group with an existing interest in supporting orphans and involved the group from the outset in planning and administering the programme' (Foster et al. 1996: 401).

For those donors and AIDS support organizations working internationally, the choice of countries to work in should be an explicit part of their scaling-up strategy. In the case of the International HIV/AIDS Alliance for example, a deliberate choice was made to work in both low-prevalence and high-prevalence countries, and in countries with both extensive and weaker NGO sectors. To a large extent, choice of countries was also influenced by the availability of donor funding.

One lesson that has emerged from NGO case studies given in this book is the value of cross-regional sharing of experiences. For example, the Alliance used lessons from approaches introduced in the Philippines to its work in Ecuador, and similarly the Salvation Army seeks explicitly to invite community members engaged in community responses to other geographic areas.

EVOLUTION OF APPROACHES TO SCALING UP AMONG DONORS AND NGO SUPPORT ORGANIZATIONS

Donors and NGO support organizations active in HIV/AIDS are not merely sources of support for NGOs' diverse approaches to scaling up, but are key players in the landscape and have a direct influence on which approaches are adopted. Yet this landscape is an extremely dynamic one, with changes in donor trends, including mechanisms and priorities for financing NGOs. For example, the past decade has seen an increasing trend to devolving funding decisions to branches or country offices based in developing countries. Similarly, following the International Conference on Population and Development in Cairo in 1994, the international emphasis was increasingly on integration of HIV/AIDS within broader reproductive health programmes with the elimination of many HIV/AIDS-specific budgets. And the creation of UNAIDS itself, with the demise of its predecessor the Global Programme of AIDS, significantly changed the nature of funding and type of support for NGO programmes in HIV/AIDS and therefore influenced their scaling-up strategies. It is likely that the creation of the Global Fund will further influence the approaches NGOs take to scaling up, although it is too early to tell in what ways.

All of the above trends are influenced by developments in technical knowledge regarding what is effective in countering HIV/AIDS; understanding of what constitutes 'best practice' is evolving particularly rapidly in HIV/AIDS. Donors, as well as responding to political concerns and accountability, reflect these technical developments. For example, interest in having an impact on the epidemic rather than simply reaching larger numbers of people or piloting initiatives, reflects both political and technical concerns. Differences of opinion remain on such issues as the relative merit of a limited number of key interventions as opposed to a 'programme approach' emphasizing a package of responses. There is also disagreement over the relative priority of working in low- versus high-prevalence countries. Finally, early approaches to the epidemic which focused on concentrating resources on so-called 'core transmitters' (groups likely to be particularly vulnerable to HIV/AIDS) are still justified by many on both efficiency and effectiveness grounds, although at the same time these are criticized because of the danger of stigmatizing such groups and missing opportunities to reach a new generation of vulnerable young people.

National government AIDS programmes' ideas about scaling up are also in flux and are influenced by such changes in international thinking, policy and funding. Their priorities, however, may differ from NGOs. Some place a strong priority on an institutional and geographic diversification of support to NGOs while maintaining a belief in 'targeted approaches' for particular populations. Others very clearly identify priority districts for increased action as well as functionally supporting particular NGOs to grow in expertise, coverage and resources. Still others appear to argue for increased support to and engagement of community groups, while challenging strong roles for national or international NGOs. These distinctions typically reflect both legitimate differences in priorities in particular places (regarding how and why to scale up action on AIDS) and inevitable differences in politics both within NGO sectors and between NGOs and governments.

Donors wishing to scale up the activities they fund for greater impact on the epidemic, then, operate in this complex and evolving policy environment. One key lesson for all concerned in scaling up is the need to anticipate changes in the donor, government and political environment over the frequently long time frame that scaling up requires. The example in Case Study 13 of the Healthy Highways project in India provides some useful insights for donors working with both NGOs and government to achieve a national impact on the epidemic.

Case Study 13 Healthy Highways (India). Coping
with policy changes over the course of scaling up

The Healthy Highways project, which developed through a complex
partnership between the UK Department for International Development (DFID), the government of India and a variety of Indian NGOs,
represents one of the most ambitious attempts to scale up an HIV/AIDS
programme to national level presented in this book. From the outset,
DFID recognized the need to engage the government of India, as it was
central to any national-scale response to HIV/AIDS. At the same time,
however, NGOs were critically important and had a comparative advantage vis-à-vis government in terms of their ability to access stigmatized
groups, to motivate behavioural change and to address the social context of HIV/AIDS. Yet NGOs – even collectively – could not claim any-
where near national coverage. A major set of challenges during the
scaling-up process was therefore this transition from scaling up NGO
contributions within their own localities to governmental ownership and
national scale without jeopardizing the strengths and sustainability of
the former. Both government and NGOs had very different perspectives
on and expectations of the scaling-up process.

The above challenges were complicated by changes in the external
policy environment in which the project proceeded, including within the
government of India and within DFID itself. There are therefore critical
lessons to be drawn for donor agencies seeking to engage in similarly
ambitious programmes with national scope, which necessarily take a
long time, and in particular those that seek to transfer their initiative to
government control while maintaining NGO involvement.

The underlying rationale for the Healthy Highways project was that
in India, where the epidemic had not yet spread into the general population, targeted interventions were key to slowing the epidemic. The
epidemiological target were the estimated 2.5 to 5 million truck-drivers
and their crew who had demonstrated potential to accelerate the
spread of HIV. Truckers were a major priority given that their mobility
throughout India made them particularly vulnerable to infection and
they were an important bridge population linking high- and low-risk
communities and geographic areas.

The scope of the project was national from its inception, aiming to
deliver three core HIV prevention strategies: behaviour change communication; condom promotion; and treatment for sexually transmitted
infections (STIs). From 1993 to 1995 consultation took place between
the key partners, including the government of India, DFID, the World

Health Organization and NGOs, as well as relevant businesses. From 1996 to 1997 the project was designed and necessary approval obtained. An 18-month pilot phase was then initiated.

In December 1997, Naz Foundation (India), based in New Delhi and established in 1994 to serve community needs that were not being met by government, conducted a study about risk behaviours among truck drivers, their crew and sexual partners. It identified myths and misconceptions concerning sexual practices, lack of treatment pro- grammes for STIs and high social stigma associated with STIs as some of the main reasons for high-risk behaviour among these groups. In response to these findings, the Naz Foundation, with the support of the Healthy Highways project, opened the Top Gear Clinic in Azadpur Transport Madni, one of the largest transportation centres in Asia. Demand for services grew so quickly that the programme had to be scaled up, with additions of counsellors and outreach staff (strategy 1, organizational expansion). The Naz programme thus successfully extended into the adjacent fruit and vegetable market centres, reach- ing men who had sex with men as well as women in nearby villages. Their own evaluations indicated that they were successful in dispelling myths and providing factual information about transmission of STIs and HIV/AIDS. Moreover, noting that most cases of unprotected sex tended to occur while under the influence of alcohol, Naz outreach staff referred cases to an addiction centre run by an NGO in New Delhi.

By the time of the completion of the pilot phase, major policy changes were afoot within both DFID and the government of India. The change of government in the UK in 1997 shifted approaches to devel- opment from direct 'aid delivery' to a greater emphasis on partnership. In turn, the government of India took a stronger role in leading the HIV/AIDS response and ensuring that major activities had to be part of a national strategy. A devolution of AIDS activities from national to state level required a reorientation of the Healthy Highways project towards an approach combining national coordination with greater state responsibility.

The above processes led to major institutional and funding changes in the Healthy Highways project's approach to scaling up. As an evalu- ation of the pilot phase achievements notes: 'The realization that resources for sustainability must primarily flow from government has been a major lesson of the pilot phase.'

These changes brought frustrations to Naz and other NGO part- ners in the project who felt they were not sufficiently consulted about the transitions and suffered from lack of funding for their own scaling up. For example, as State AIDS Control societies started to take over the project in phases, under new guidelines the doctors' salaries would be cut in half and medicines initially distributed free of cost were charged to the clients. For Naz itself, financial constraints were the greatest constraint to their scaling up, and meant they lacked resources to train additional community outreach workers or to increase condom distribution outlets.

A former DFID employee involved in this project concludes in hindsight that one of the greatest pitfalls in this scaling-up process, despite its notable successes, was that the scaling up was not sufficiently planned and resourced accordingly. Scaling up as transition requires clear objectives, indicators for achieving the transition and a plan of activities. In addition, it requires a system of monitoring and adjusting the plan of activities according to unforeseen changes in the overall policy environment, including time and opportunities for reflection during implementation.

A very positive development over the past several years, partly inspired by the greater international commitment to HIV/AIDS witnessed internationally, is an increased awareness among donors of the complementarities between different organizations' investments and of the synergies between different interventions (UNAIDS 2000a). As discussed earlier, it is too soon to assess the impact on HIV/AIDS of sector-wide approaches to the health sector in developing countries. It may be that the greater recognition, implicit in such new modalities of providing overseas aid, of the need for such aid to complement and support national directives will have a positive impact.

Donors' and NGO support organizations' priorities in supporting the scaling up of NGOs' programmes in HIV/AIDS have shifted significantly since the beginning of the epidemic, as political circumstances have changed and technical knowledge about the disease has increased. Examples abound of where a lack of sufficient support for the entire scaling-up process has led to a 'feast-and-famine' approach by NGOs. Supporting the scaling-up process requires not only a higher level of resources but also greater understanding of the complexities of scaling up and that institutional questions are not merely a 'delivery cost' of increasing the scale of given interventions. There is a danger that increasing and indiscriminate pressure on NGOs to scale up their programmes in HIV/AIDS will undermine the comparative advantage of some NGOs or strengthen individual programmes of NGOs at the expense of others. On the other hand, strengthening those elements of institutional capacity in which NGOs have traditionally been weak – such as evaluation or generating costing information – could considerably enhance the ability of NGOs to direct their own programmes for maximum impact.

Conclusion

From the early days of the epidemic, NGOs joined epidemiologists within the HIV/AIDS field in warning of its potential devastation. Nevertheless, it was not until some 20 years later at the dawn of the 21st century that prevailing international discourse about HIV/AIDS moved from seeing the problem as primarily a disease affecting marginalized social groups to recognizing that it is a global pandemic affecting every sector of society. The creation in 2001 of the Global Fund for AIDS, Tuberculosis and Malaria represented a belated acknowledgement that HIV/AIDS is no longer perceived as a medical problem, but rather as a major development challenge.

New levels and channels of funding for HIV/AIDS have been stimulating inquiry into the best means of responding to the epidemic on a large enough scale to have an impact on its progression and to alleviate some of the individual tragedies and social upheaval it brings. The urgency of expanding the scale of existing programmes in prevention, care and support and finding new ways to reach those who are vulnerable is finally recognized. In itself, this shift in international commitment is a positive step forward for NGOs active in HIV/AIDS, but it also poses new challenges as to how this funding can be spent most appropriately. In effect, NGOs are facing a dual pressure, both from the rapidly advancing epidemic itself, as well as increasing emphasis internationally on scaling up activities.

This need to examine whether organizations active in HIV/AIDS have done enough in thinking about scaling up their impact applies across the board, and not only to NGOs. Governments, arguably, have the greatest responsibility to reach their entire populations and to provide the leadership that creates a conducive moral and political environment in which HIV/AIDS activities can be carried out. So-called success stories in HIV/AIDS have been seen as such precisely because effective government action was taken early on in the course of the epidemics in those countries. The private sector, too, cannot ignore HIV/AIDS and the ethical issues it raises without thinking more systematically about how it can work on HIV/AIDS with those they employ, their families and their communities. NGOs, however, have led the way in dealing with the epidemic humanely and effectively in many developing countries. Both internationally and nationally, they have pioneered many of the most influential elements of an appropriate response to the epidemic. The diverse successes of NGOs active in HIV/AIDS have shaped public discourse on, and ways of approaching, the epidemic with their understanding of its social context and with their particular attention to its ethical and human rights implications. As examples throughout this book have shown, NGOs have been at the forefront of advocacy to reduce discrimination and stigma, increased access to treatment, and pilot programmes to test out possible interventions and contribute to sharing best practice which others have then integrated. In many cases, the success of their scaling up has been premised on allying with other social movements such as those concerned with gender relations or human rights. As Helen Schneider notes of the contribution of NGOs in South Africa:

> Underlying the power of non-governmental actors is their access to both cultural and social capital, generated by the linking of multiple social dimensions and spaces: marginalised gay men and township youth; middle class expertise and popular mobilisation; individual and broader social and economic rights; activists and scientists; the North and the South; the national and the international

> *(Schneider 2002: 162).*

As this quotation clearly illustrates, none of these types of institution can themselves, acting alone, make a dent in the epidemic or alleviate its effects. Partnerships are essential, as discussed extensively in Chapter 6, and indeed most patterns of scaling up described in the book have assumed some relationship with other types of institution, whether they be governments, services, CBOs or research institutions. Such alliances are often time-consuming and need to surmount inevitable differences in institutional culture and in defining priorities, but as examples in this book have shown, they can bring high rewards.

NGOs are also facing the challenge that their role not only in HIV/AIDS but in social development more broadly is being re-examined. Over the past two decades at least, NGOs in developing countries have been the recipients of enormous international attention and resources, and have been praised by both the political left and political right. In many ways, however, that 'honeymoon' period is over, in that critical voices are questioning the impact of NGOs and why they have not increased the scale of their activities. While recognizing the many micro-level successes of NGOs across sectors of development activity, these sceptics have argued that NGOs rarely invest in the means to evaluate their own effectiveness. More worryingly, many NGOs have become more accountable to international funding agencies than to the beneficiaries they aim to assist. Therefore scaling such organizations up further is only likely to increase this social distance between NGOs and the communities they work with.

However, if NGOs are urged to increase their impact and scale up their activities, this may lead to a number of associated risks. These include the danger that their comparative advantage of being responsive to local communities, flexible and able to adapt to changing circumstances, may be undermined. Increased size may be associated with greater bureaucracy and more professionalism, but with losses in terms of the quality of human relationships and ability to motivate social change. Moreover, there has been relatively little systematic attention to the question of *how* NGOs might go about deliberately scaling up without such attendant risks.

The general challenge of scaling up NGO activity is all the more complex in the field of HIV/AIDS because of its sensitivity and the pervasive stigma associated with it. Despite their strengths, NGOs active in HIV/AIDS have, for a variety of reasons, faced considerable obstacles, but have also been reluctant to scale up their existing programmes in HIV/AIDS. NGOs themselves may blame inadequate donor support as one of the key reasons for this state of affairs. Certainly evidence in the book has shown that donors often do not understand the complexity of scaling up nor plan their support to anticipate the demands that scaling up places on both the organization concerned and its programmes. Nonetheless, there are a variety of other challenges which are just as salient. HIV/AIDS-related NGOs share the widespread fear, noted above, that scaling up local responses will bureaucratize them, ultimately undermining the comparative NGO advantage in motivating behavioural change and supporting HIV-affected communities at close hand. Many NGOs active in HIV/AIDS fear that scaling up their programmes will result in a deterioration in quality, despite the fact that few have institutionalized mechanisms for measuring the quality of their own programmes. In other cases, there is concern that scaling up work with marginalized communities may bring greater visibility – and possibly social prejudice and AIDS-related stigma – to these groups. Finally, communities affected by HIV/AIDS are already responding in their own ways to the epidemic, and organizations such as FACT/FOCUS and the Salvation Army among others are seeking to build on these efforts. These and other NGOs argue therefore that external agencies such as NGOs need to understand and support these initiatives rather than always focusing on expanding their own action to deliver larger programmes to communities.

Despite the above concerns, however, many NGOs have already scaled up their HIV/AIDS activities in a myriad of ways. NGOs' experiences illustrate that scaling up is more complex than simply scaling up evidence-based interventions through replication or expansion. NGOs may draw on some of the concrete examples of ways in which organizations from across the world have approached scaling up their impact in many more ways than organizational expansion alone. These have stretched across the spectrum of HIV/AIDS programmes from prevention to clinical services to care and support for orphans. They have also encompassed a range of strategies, including organizational expansion (strategy 1), catalysing others' response to HIV/AIDS (strategy 2), diffusion of innovative concepts or approaches (strategy 3), influencing policy through advocacy (strategy 4) and mainstreaming HIV/AIDS into development (strategy 5). Arguably the greater prominence HIV/AIDS now carries on the international policy agenda is due to the successful advocacy activities of civil society movements concerned about the inequities the epidemic displays. The above scaling-up strategies have often been employed together, or have shifted over time as the environment of the NGO changes, the policy context shifts or because of the insights gained over time by the organizations involved.

One of the first lessons that emerges from this collective experience of NGOs scaling up their programmes documented in this book is the importance of explicit discussion of the objectives and approach to scaling up by all concerned. Definitions of scaling up vary according to one's institutional perspective and approach to HIV/AIDS, and therefore clarifying potential misunderstandings or conflicts in perspective is a critical first step (see Chapter 2). As the executive director of the International HIV/AIDS Alliance, Jeff O'Malley, articulates, such discussion among those who are involved in scaling up in advance may pre-empt many problems occurring later:

> The Alliance was established within a rhetoric of 'scaling up community responses to AIDS'. What did that mean to different stakeholders? If more

attention had been paid to the phrase, more contradictions in approach
amongst and within different sets of stakeholders would have been identified.

However, while definitions of scaling up vary according to the perspective of the individual and the organization, consensus exists over
the need to define objectives in terms of impact on either preventing
the epidemic or mitigating its effects. A narrow understanding of
impact, however, based only on reducing the number of new infections without looking at the synergies between prevention, care and
support, and the broader social change needed to address HIV/AIDS,
is misleading. NGOs, based on the many successful, but often undoc-
umented, experiences of scaling up, need to articulate their own
notions of the impact of their efforts, and to communicate these to a
broader audience. This would include evaluating their work in terms
of overall levels of HIV/AIDS-related needs in the populations they
serve, rather than only in relation to their own capacity.

NGOs may have to sacrifice some elements of the quality of the
programmes they run for the sake of broader coverage. Yet at the same
time, it is critical that they have the institutional capacity to evaluate
the quality of their own programmes and thus be able to identify if
and when it declines. ASI in Guatemala, for example, was able to identify that although it was able to offer testing and counselling to more
people through its expansion, many were not returning for their test
results, and this prompted a revision of the scaling-up strategy.

The foregoing chapters have also underscored that scaling up necessarily occurs over time and thus objectives or needs may be
dynamic throughout this process. Scaling up entails, in some cases,
expanding coverage, in others, altering the type or intensity of coverage, but in still other cases or stages of the process the focus may
be on increasing impact or improving quality. For example, the scaling-up initiative of the Family Health Trust's Anti-AIDS Clubs in
Zambia was primarily through revitalizing and improving the quality
of an initiative that was already operating at considerable scale. One
of the lessons of the Healthy Highways project in India was the need
for the actors involved in the scaling up to be able to adapt to
changes in the external policy environment.

Another lesson emerging from the experience documented here is
that much more information is needed on how costs change over time
through scaling up. As discussed in Chapter 7, such data are rare in general, but particularly lacking concerning NGO programmes. Both the
prevailing culture and priorities of NGOs do not favour the collection

of such data and they may be uncomfortable with the associated need to quantify impact. However, it is important that NGOs learn the techniques economists use both to increase their own bargaining power with funding and other agencies, and also to increase their own efficiency in reaching their proclaimed objectives. This information can be useful to NGOs as one of many criteria used to decide whether and how to approach scaling up in the context of constrained resources.

NGOs, donors and NGO support organizations need to recognize that it is not appropriate for all NGOs to scale up and nor should NGOs scale up all of their activities simultaneously. In any one country, a range of institutional responses is needed, and thus it is critical that not only NGOs, but also governments, the private sector and donors have an understanding of the inter-relationship and comparative advantage of these actors. With the increased level of resources available in the field, there is a very real danger of swamping a few organizations with good reputations and imposing unrealistic expectations on them. Similarly, within given organizations, choices as to which aspects of an NGO's work to scale up with maximum impact have to be made carefully and take into consideration the potential synergies between different types of intervention.

As the third part of the book argues, paying attention to building institutional capacity of NGOs is not merely a 'delivery cost' of implementing large-scale interventions but is fundamental to the sustainability of scaling up the response to HIV/AIDS. Ideally, political and funding environments would allow NGOs to be proactive in scaling up, with sufficient time for reflection and planning in order to maximize impact and safeguard their organizational mission. If they are merely responding to donor demands or the evolution of the epidemic, they will command little control over the scaling-up process and ultimately perhaps have less effect. To the extent that is possible, NGOs need to prepare their own staff and structures for the scaling up process which, as discussed extensively in Chapter 4, is likely to change the nature of decision-making, of staffing and of relationships within organizations. The experience of KANCO was instructive as one of the few organizations cited in the book which paid considerable attention to the organizational development issues associated with scaling up. Finding an appropriate balance between attending to internal as opposed to programmatic concerns is a critical challenge in scaling up.

Finally, a major lesson of the experiences of scaling up has been the need for public and other types of services to keep pace with NGO expansion. A critical constraint on the scaling-up efforts of NGOs documented in this book as their programmes expand, in high-prevalence settings particularly, has been the weak capacity of existing health services and the insufficient availability of HIV-related commodities, including drugs and condoms. In turn, it is unethical for NGOs to raise demand for services provided by other institutions when the latter are ill-equipped to deal with that need.

There is, therefore, much more that NGOs can do to address the HIV/AIDS epidemic at a larger scale than they have already. This is particularly the case in the current international context with belated recognition of the implications of the global pandemic and new resources available to fight it. As reiterated throughout the book, however, NGOs cannot do so alone. Government commitment and leadership are essential if all institutions responding to the worst epidemic in human history are to be encouraged to do their work effectively.

List of workshop participants

Paurvi Bhatt
(at that time)
USAID/DC
G/PHN/HN/HIV-AIDS
Washington DC , USA

Ian Campbell
International HQ
Salvation Army
London, UK

Chris Castle
Horizons/International
    HIV/AIDS Alliance
Washington DC, USA

Phyllis Craun-Selka
PACT
Washington DC, USA

Jocelyn DeJong
Institute for Development
    Policy and Management
University of Manchester
Manchester, UK

Thom Eisele
Tulane University
New Orleans, USA

Geoff Foster
Family AIDS Caring Trust
Zimbabwe

Naomi Gonahasa
TASO
Uganda

Gail Goodridge
Family Health International
Arlington, USA

Baba Goumbala
ANCS
Dakar, Senegal

Robert Grose
DFID
London, UK

Annelise Hirschmann
ASI (AGPCS)
Guatemala

Dixter Kaluba
Family Health Trust
Lusaka, Zambia

Lilani Kumaranayake
London School of Hygiene and
    Tropical Medicine
Department of Public Health &
    Policy
London, UK

Tim Lee
International HIV/AIDS Alliance
Brighton, UK

Hor Bun Leng
NCHADS
Phnom Penh, Cambodia

Ruthy Libatique
PHANSuP
Quezon City, Philippines

Sue Lucas
International HIV/AIDS Alliance
Brighton, UK

Rita Marima-Muyambo
Project Support Group
Harare, Zimbabwe

Issam Moussaoui
PASA/IST-SIDA
c/o AMSED
Rabat, Morocco

Shyamala Nataraj
SIAAP
Adyar, India

Jeff O'Malley
International HIV/AIDS Alliance
Brighton, UK

Kevin Orr
International HIV/AIDS Alliance
Brighton, UK

Pok Panhavichetr
KHANA
Phnom Penh, Cambodia

Helen Parry
International HIV/AIDS Alliance
Brighton, UK

Elizabeth Pisani
Consultant
UNAIDS
Nairobi, Kenya

Margarita Quevedo
Corporacion KIMIRINA
Quito, Ecuador

Allan Ragi
KANCO
Nairobi, Kenya

C. Ramachandran
SIAAP
Chennai
Tamil Nadu, India

Naomi Rutenberg
Population Council/Horizons
Washington DC, USA

Marie-Rose Sawadogo
IPC – BP
Ouagadougou, Burkina Faso

Glossary

Advocacy: process to bring about change in the attitudes, practices, policies and laws of influential individuals, groups and institutions, carried out by people proposing improvements on behalf of themselves or others.

Antiretroviral therapies: treatment to reduce the amount of replicating virus to as low a level as possible, thereby preventing infection of new cells and further damage to the immune system.

Asymptomatic: infected by a disease agent but not exhibiting any medical symptoms.

Care and support: efforts that aim to improve the quality of life and life expectancy of people living with HIV/AIDS and persons affected by HIV/AIDS.

Community-based organization (CBO): group and association formed by people living within specific communities that work at the local level, and mostly seek to ensure benefits for their members. CBOs do not always require formal procedures, such as legal registration.

Condom promotion: to encourage the use of a type of prophylactic that can prevent sexually transmitted infections and AIDS.

Core transmitters: a term used by some to denote groups likely to be particularly vulnerable to HIV/AIDS.

Evidence-based interventions: the conscientious, explicit and judicious use of current best evidence about effectiveness in making decisions about public health interventions.

Female condom: a strong, soft, transparent polyurethane sheath inserted into the vagina before sexual intercourse, providing protection against both pregnancy and sexually transmitted diseases. It forms a barrier between the penis and the vagina, cervix and external genitalia.

Global Fund to Fight AIDS, Tuberculosis, and Malaria: the Global Fund is an independent, public–private partnership working to increase funding to fight AIDS, TB and malaria on a global level and to direct these funds to effective prevention and treatment programmes in the countries with greatest need.

Harm reduction: a set of practical strategies that reduce negative consequences of injected drug use; these include a range from safer use to managed use to abstinence. Harm reduction can encompass programmes in education, counselling, drug substitution or needle exchange as examples.

High-risk behaviour: activities that increase a person's risk of transmitting or becoming infected with a disease.

Microbicides: products intended for vaginal or rectal administration that can decrease the transmission of HIV and other microorganisms causing sexually transmitted infections.

Peer education: this typically involves the use of members of a given group to effect change among other members of the same group. Peer education is used to effect change at the individual level by attempting to modify a person's knowledge, attitudes, beliefs and behaviours. However, peer education can also effect change at a group or societal level by modifying norms and stimulating collective action that leads to changes in programmes and policies.

Person affected by HIV/AIDS: those living with a person living with HIV/AIDS (PLHA) (wife/husband/partner, children, parents, brothers/sisters, grandparents, etc.); those who are part of the close circle of a PLHA but not living with them; those who are personally involved in the care and support of one or more PLHA. The definition used therefore excludes people who provide care and support to PLHA in a professional capacity.

Prevention: that which aims to prevent the transmission of HIV from people infected with the virus to non-infected people as well as the reinfection of those who are already HIV-positive.

Prevalence: the percentage of persons in a given population with a disease or condition at a given point in time.

Prevalence of HIV: the number of people with HIV at a point in time, often expressed as a percentage of the total population.

Sexually transmitted infections: infectious diseases spread from person to person through direct body contact or contact with infected body fluids. The term is used to describe any disease acquired primarily through sexual contact.

Social marketing of condoms: programmes designed to raise condom use by improving the social acceptability of condoms, making them more widely available through non-traditional outlets and offering them for sale at subsidized prices.

Surveillance: close or continuous observation or testing (e.g. serosurveillance), used in epidemiology for example. Immunological surveillance, or immunosurveillance, is monitoring of the immune system that detects and destroys neoplastic (e.g. cancerous) cells and that tends to break down in immunosuppressed individuals.

Sentinel surveillance: surveillance conducted through 'watch post' sites that provide access to populations that are of particular interest or representative of a larger population.

Serosurveillance: epidemiological study or activity based on the detection through serological testing of presence or absence of HIV antibody. Latent, subclinical infections and carrier states can thus be detected, in addition to clinically overt cases.

Stigma (AIDS-related) or stigma towards people living with HIV/AIDS: several authors (e.g. Brown et al. 2001) divide stigma into *felt* or *perceived* stigma and *enacted* stigma. Felt stigma refers to real or imagined fear of societal attitudes and potential discrimination arising from a particular undesirable attribute or disease (such as HIV), or association with a particular group. For example, an individual may deny his or her risk of HIV infection, refuse to use condoms or refuse to disclose HIV status for fear of the possible negative reactions of family, friends and community. Felt stigma may be a survival strategy to limit the occurrence of enacted stigma. Enacted stigma refers to the real experience of discrimination. For example, the disclosure of an individual's HIV-positive status leads to loss of a job or social ostracism.

Targeted approaches or targeting interventions: the purpose of targeting is to reach intended clients with a particular intervention, message or resource. Targeting should not be confused with a narrow focus or limited scope. Even interventions intended for a broad audience, e.g. the 'general' population, need to be properly targeted. Targeting helps to ensure that the intended audience is actually exposed to the message, understands the message and has the information needed to appropriately respond to the message. Targeting should also not be confused with prioritization. All interventions should be targeted, but not all potential interventions have the same priority. Prioritization relates to the importance of the population or behaviour in terms of their current or potential role in the epidemic, while targeting helps to define how best to reach that population or address that behaviour.

Vulnerability: those features of a social group or economic entity that make it more likely that excess morbidity and mortality associated with disease will have negative effects. Vulnerability is influenced by a wide range of factors including personal, such as the ability to protect oneself, and societal, such as cultural norms.

Endnotes

1 All statistics cited in this book on the HIV/AIDS epidemic are from UNAIDS (2002a).
2 Specifically, Medecins Sans Frontieres has launched an international campaign since 1999 to lower the prices of existing drugs, bring abandoned drugs back into production, stimulate research and development for diseases that primarily affect the poor, and overcome other barriers to access (see www.accessmed-msf.org).
3 These rules were laid down in 1994 on the premise of protecting intellectual property rights in a globalized era when information and technologies flow more easily across national borders. They were embodied in the controversial agreement entitled Trade-Related Aspects of Intellectual Property Rights (TRIPS).
4 Nonetheless, the contribution of the US government of only $500 million over three years will include funds taken from existing international health programmes, including those for maternal and child health in developing countries (Epstein and Chen 2002).
5 Refer to glossary.
6 Horizons/Alliance Seminar on Scaling Up, Windsor, England, 1–5 September 2000. A list of participants in that workshop and their affiliations is provided in the Appendix.
7 'Boutique' projects are small-scale, often pilot projects to which a high level of resources may be allocated and which act as a showcase for particular approaches, but which may not be sustainable at a greater scale.
8 For an argument that HIV/AIDS should not be granted special status because of these ethical and rights concerns, and should be confronted with more of the 'traditional tools of public health' in the context of the US (see Burr 1997).
9 This debate echoes that about child health in the 1980s when there were calls in some quarters for the implementation of selective technical interventions known to be effective in combating childhood diarrhoeal disease, for example. These were countered by others, who argued that the social factors leading to disease, such as poverty and poor sanitation, must be addressed (see Rifkin and Walt 1988).
10 Arguably, however, if treatment and support were provided to those with HIV, prevention efforts would be more successful.

11 Or, in the words of the local response team at UNAIDS, making 'AIDS-competent societies'.

12 Of the 13 case studies of scaling up NGO activities presented at the Horizons/Alliance Scaling Up Seminar, only three explicitly addressed costs – the Project Support Group in Zimbabwe, the Government–NGO collaboration for Home Care in Cambodia and the International HIV/AIDS Alliance.

13 Foster and others note that these community initiatives are more likely to emerge in care and support than prevention, as will be discussed below.

14 For example, SIAAP, which was operating with 40 employees, cut its staff down to only six prior to a subsequent 're-scaling'.

15 This is the case in Ecuador, for example, according to the director of KIMIRINA.

16 This discussion draws on Korten 1980 and Myers 1992.

17 *Who Changes?* by Blackburn and Holland (1998), inspired by Robert Chambers' work, entails a series of case studies of increasing the scale of the practice of participatory rapid assessment precisely through this approach.

18 See Edwards and Hulme 1992, 1996, 1997.

19 This has also been referred to as 'grafting', whereby, for example, a programme for adolescents is added to existing services that failed to reach adolescents (Smith and Colvin 2000) and could also apply to links with governmental services.

20 Other examples of such types of organization include TASO and SIAAP.

21 This was one of the conclusions of the UK NGO AIDS Consortium report 1996.

22 The HIV/AIDS Alliance conducted participatory assessments in 1994–95 on the needs of local AIDS service NGOs in 12 developing countries, and found that: 'The NGOs surveyed in most of the countries also cited the need for more action on the contextual (societal) factors which increase vulnerability to HIV, such as gender inequality' (O'Malley et al. 1996: 346).

23 This example is from the case study of the International HIV/AIDS Alliance in UNAIDS with Local Business Council (2000) (The Business Response to HIV/AIDS).

24 This example is drawn from UNAIDS with Local Business Council (2000) (The Business Response to HIV/AIDS).

25 Based on the experience of the author working in Egypt, 1992–99.

26 Uvin and Miller (1996) refer to 'push' factors for scaling up which are largely supply-driven – that is, where the impetus for scaling up comes from the programme providers themselves, usually NGOs or government; and 'pull' factors where demands for scaling up emerge from the recipients or participants of the intervention programme. Nonetheless, there is a need to further disaggregate these categories. Moreover, in practice, expansion is likely to result from a combination of motivations.

27   See, for example, Horizons consultation report entitled 'Integrating HIV Prevention and Care into Maternal and Child Healthcare Settings: Lessons Learned from Horizons Studies', July 2001. The Horizons web site can be accessed via the Population Council web site (www.popcouncil.org).

28   Their actual epidemiological risk has not been studied. C. Ramachandran of SIAAP notes that they may be at high risk because they tend to marry later, and often live in hostels or institutions for the blind (personal communication).

29   I am grateful to Stefano Bertozzi of the Instituto Nacional de Salud Publica (Mexico) for this insight.

30   We are grateful to Lilani Kumaranayake of the London School of Hygiene and Tropical Medicine for providing the material in this chapter.

31   For this point, I am grateful to Stefano Bertozzi (op.cit.).

32   Cost considerations presented in this chapter are restricted to those from an institutional perspective of the NGO involved in scaling up and its partners; costing from the perspective of beneficiaries raises a separate but important set of issues.

33   The dynamics created in PWHA organizations by greater donor funds being made available are particularly complex given the fact of the intrinsic conflict of interest where staff and beneficiaries belong to the same group (O'Malley et al. 1996).

34   Geoffrey Woolcock and Dennis Altman cited in O'Malley et al. (1996). This has also been found in Brazil, where the fact that a World Bank project brought an increasing scale of funding to NGOs made them less critical of government policy (according to Richard Parker and Jane Galvao, as cited by Chris Castle, personal communication).

35   A report commissioned by USAID on measuring absorptive capacity within the population and health field (Brown et al. 2000) notes that the available literature suggests that efforts to measure the outcomes of capacity-building are at a very early stages of development, although there is a wealth of experience described in the grey literature. The availability to developing country organizations of the latter literature, which documents, for example, a range of measures for self-assessment of organizational capacity, is unclear.

36   Information from Monthly HIV Update, April 2002.

37   J Decosas (1994) 'The answer to AIDS lies in united commitment', *AIDS Analysis Africa* 5(1): 3–4, quoted in Campbell and Williams 1999.

38   See for example Nnko (1998) on Tanzania.

39   For example, Klouda (1995) cites a study in Abidjan which found that 26% of patients from the lowest socio-economic group reported having been rejected, blamed or isolated by their families as opposed to none in the highest socio-economic group.

40   Bob Grose, UK Department for International Development, who was formerly involved in the Healthy Highways project (see Case Study 13).

41   This risk has been cited by Woolcock and Altman in O'Malley et al. (1996) in the case of Australia.

42 Smith and Colvin (2000) analyse this point extensively in relation to adolescent services.

43 Lilani Kumanarayake (personal communication) notes from her experience with colleagues trying to estimate the impact of NGO prevention activities in a number of countries that even routine monitoring of measures such as the number of people being reached may not always occur.

44 I am grateful to David Hulme of the Institute for Development Policy and Management, University of Manchester, for suggesting this 'portfolio' approach.

References

Ainsworth, M. and Teokul, W., Breaking the silence: setting realistic priorities for AIDS control in less-developed countries, *Lancet*, Vol. 356, 2000, pp.55–60.

Antivelink, L., Abaliio, A., Byateesa, D., Gonahasa, N., Kabanda, M., Kajura, C., Lukwago, B., Mike, J., Mwiri, M., Shillingi, L., Ssebbanja, P., Watuwa, S., with Mwesigwa, J., Osuga, B., Cooper, R. and Welbourn, A. (1996) A Participatory Approach to a Mid-Term Review: the AIDS Support Organisation (TASO) Community-Based Care Programme, Uganda, unpublished mimeo, July, and forthcoming in Cornwall, A. and Welbourn, A., *Listening to Learn: Participatory Approaches to Sexual and Reproductive Health*, Zed Books, London.

Asthana, S. and Oostvogels, R., Community participation in HIV prevention: problems and prospects for community-based strategies among female sex workers in Madras, *Social Science and Medicine*, Vol. 43(2), 1996, pp.133–48.

Avina, J., The evolutionary life cycles of non-governmental development organizations, *Public Administration and Development*, Vol. 13, 1993, pp.453–74.

Billis, D. and MacKeith, J. (1992) Growth and change in NGOs: concepts and comparative experience, in Edwards, M. and Hulme, D. (eds), *Making a Difference: NGOs and Development in a Changing World*, Earthscan Publications, London. pp.118–27.

Binswanger, H., Scaling up HIV/AIDS programs to national coverage, *Science*, Vol. 288, 2000, pp.2173–6.

Blackburn, J. and Holland, J. (1998) *Who Changes? Institutionalizing participation in Development*, ITDG Publishing, London.

Boyce, W., Johnston, C., Thomas, M., Enns, H., Naidu, D.M. and Tjandrakusm, H., Pathways to scaling-up in community based rehabilitation agencies, *International Journal of Rehabilitation Research*, Vol. 20, 1997, pp.381–92.

Bratton, M. (1989) The politics of government–NGO relations in Africa, *World Development*, Vol. 17(4), 1989, pp.569–87.

Brown, L., LaFond, A. and Macintyre, K. (2000) Measuring Capacity Building, MEASURE Evaluation Project, unpublished draft.

Brown, L., Trujillo, L., and Macintyre, K. (2001) *Interventions to Reduce HIV/AIDS Stigma: what have we learned?* Horizons and Tulane University, p.4.

Burr, C., The AIDS exception: privacy vs. public health, *Atlantic Monthly*, June 1997.

Campbell, C. and Williams, B., Beyond the biomedical and behavioural: towards an integrated approach to HIV prevention in the Southern African mining industry, *Social Science and Medicine*, Vol. 48, 1999, pp.1625–39.

Chambers, R. (1992) Spreading and self-improving: a strategy for scaling up, in Edwards, M. and Hulme, D. (eds), *Making a Difference: NGOs and Development in a Changing World*, Earthscan Publications, London, pp.40–9.

Charlton, R., Sustaining an impact? Development NGOs in the 1990s, *Third World Quarterly*, Vol. 16(3), 1995, pp.566–75.

Clark, J. (1991) *Democratizing Development: the Role of Voluntary Organizations*, Kumarian Press, Connecticut.

Clark, J. (1992) Policy influence, lobbying and advocacy, in Edwards, M. and Hulme, D. (eds), *Making a Difference: NGOs and Development in a Changing World*, Earthscan Publications, London, pp.191–203.

Decosas, J., The answer to AIDS lies in united commitment, *AIDS Analysis Africa*, Vol. 5(1), 1994, pp.3–4.

Decosas, J., The local response to HIV in Africa: a question of scale, *AIDS Analysis Africa*, Vol. 10(5), 2000.

DeJong, J. (2000) 'The Challenge of Increasing the Scale of Non-Governmental Organizations' HIV/AIDS Efforts in Developing Countries', unpublished draft, University of Manchester, UK.

Drabek, A.G., Development alternatives: the challenge for NGOs – an overview of the issues, *World Development*, Vol. 15 (supplement), 1987, pp.ix–xv.

Edwards, M. and Hulme, D. (1992) *Making a Difference: NGOs And Development in a Changing World*, Earthscan Publications, London.

Edwards, M. and Hulme, D. (1996) *Beyond the Magic Bullet: NGO Performance and Accountability in the post-Cold War World*, Kumarian Press, Connecticut.

Edwards, M. and Hulme, D. (1997) *NGOs, States and Donors: too close for comfort?* Macmillan Press, London.

Eisele, T. (2000) *Going to Scale in HIV/AIDS Programs: A Review of Current Literature*, Tulane University, New Orleans, Louisiana.

Epstein, H., AIDS: the lesson of Uganda, *New York Review of Books*, 5 July, 2001, pp.18–23.

Epstein, H. and Chen, L., Can AIDS be stopped? *New York Review of Books*, 14 March, 2002, pp.29–31.

Evans, C. (1999) *An International Review of the Rationale, Role and Evaluation of Community Development Approaches in Interventions to Reduce HIV Transmission in Sex Work*, Horizons, New Delhi.

Forsythe, S., Arthur, G., Ngatia, G., Mutemi, R., Odhiambo, J. and Gilks, C., Assessing the cost and willingness to pay for voluntary HIV counselling and testing in Kenya, *Health Policy and Planning*, Vol. 17(2), 2002, pp.187–95.

Foster, G., Makufa, C., Drew, R., Kambeu, S. and Saurombe, K., Supporting children in need through a community-based orphan visiting programme, *AIDS Care*, Vol. 8(4), 1996, pp.389–403.

Fowler, A., The role of NGOs in changing state-society relations: perspectives from Eastern and Southern Africa, *Development Policy Review*, Vol. 9, 1991, pp.53–84.

Gilmore, N. and Somerville, M., Stigmatization, scapegoating and discrimination in sexually transmitted diseases: overcoming 'them' and 'us', *Social Science and Medicine*, Vol. 39(9), 1994, pp.1339–58.

Gilson, L., Sen, P.D., Mohammed, S. and Muljinja, P., The potential of health sector non-governmental organizations: policy options, *Health Policy and Planning*, Vol. 9(1), 1994, pp.14–24.

Goldin, C.S., Stigmatization and AIDS: critical issues in public health, *Social Science and Medicine*, Vol. 39(9), 1994, pp.1359–66.

Health Watch (1998) From Contraceptive Targets to Reproductive Health: India's Family Planning Program after Cairo, unpublished case study prepared for Health, Empowerment, Rights and Accountability (HERA) meeting in Cocoyoc, Mexico, November 1998.

Herek, G., AIDS and stigma, *American Behavioral Scientist*, Vol. 42(7), 1999, pp.1106–16.

Hodson, R. (1992) Small, medium or large? The rocky road to NGO growth, in Edwards, M. and Hulme, D. (eds), *Making a Difference: NGOs and Development in a Changing World*, Earthscan Publications, London. pp.127–37.

Horizons (2000a) *Case Studies on Scaling Up*, Horizons, Washington, DC.

Horizons (2000b) Going to Scale in HIV/AIDS Programs: A Review of Current Literature, unpublished document developed by Horizons in collaboration with Tulane University.

Horizons (2000c) *Peer Education and HIV/AIDS: Past Experience, Future Directions*, Horizons/Population Council, New York.

Howes, M. and Sattar, M.G. (1992) Bigger and better? Scaling up strategies pursued by BRAC 1972–1991, in Edwards, M. and Hulm, D. (eds), *Making a Difference: NGOs and Development in a Changing World*, Earthscan Publications, London. pp.99–111.

Hughes, H., Evaluating HIV/AIDS programmes, *Development in Practice*, Vol. 3(1), 1993, pp.52–4.

Hyden, G. and Lanegran, K., Eastern Africa: mapping the politics of AIDS, *AIDS and Society*, Vol. 2(2), 1991, pp.1, 6, 12–13.

International HIV/AIDS Alliance and GlaxoSmithKline in Global Partnership with HIV/AIDS Communities (2000a) Community Lessons, Global Learning Project, unpublished report of Zambia meeting.

International HIV/AIDS Alliance and GlaxoSmithKline in Global Partnership with HIV/AIDS Communities (2000b) Community Lessons, Global Learning Project, unpublished report of India meeting.

International HIV/AIDS Alliance and GlaxoSmithKline in Global Partnership with HIV/AIDS Communities (2001) *Expanding Community Action on HIV/AIDS: NGO/CBO Strategies for Scaling-up*, London.

Jareg, P. and Kaseje, D.C.O., Growth of civil society in developing countries: implications for health, *Lancet*, Vol. 351, 1998, p.819.

Kaleeba, N., Kalibala, S., Kaseje Ssebbanja, P., Anderson, S., van Praag, E., Tembo, G. and Katabira, E., Participatory evaluation of counseling, medical and social services of The Aids Support Organization (TASO) in Uganda, *AIDS*, Vol. 9(1), 1997, pp.13–26.

Klouda, T., Responding to AIDS: are there any appropriate development and health policies? *Journal of International Development*, Vol. 7(3), 1995, pp.467–87.

Korten, D.C., Community organizations and rural development: a learning process approach, *Public Administration Review*, Sept/Oct, 1980, pp.480–511.

Kumaranayake, L. (2000) *The Economics of Scaling-Up*, paper presented at WHO Commission on Macroeconomics and Health Planning Meeting for Working Group 05.00, London School of Hygiene and Tropical Medicine.

Kumaranayake, L. and Watts, C. (2000a) *The Costs of Scaling-up HIV Prevention and Care Interventions in Sub-Saharan Africa*, XIII International AIDS Conference, Durban, July 2000. Abstract [TuOrD324].

Kumaranayake, L. and Watts, C., Economist costs of HIV/AIDS prevention activities in sub-Saharan Africa, *AIDS*, Vol. 14 (Supplement 3), 2000b, pp.S239–S252.

Kumaranayake, L., Pepperall, J., Goodman, H., Mills, A. and Walker, D. (2000) *Costing Guidelines for HIV/AIDS Prevention Strategies, UNAIDS Best Practice Collection* – key materials, UNAIDS, Geneva.

Lenton, C. (1993) The International Alliance Supporting Community Action on AIDS (IASCAA) Proposal for Support, 12 November.

Loughran, L., Capacity building for HIV/AIDS prevention, *AIDS Captions*, Vol. II(2), 1995, pp.4–7.

Mayhew, S., Integrating MCh/FP and STD/HIV services: current debates and future directions, *Health Policy and Planning*, Vol. 11(4), 1996, pp.339–53.

Myers, R. (1992) Going to scale, in Cooperson, W. (ed.), *The Twelve Who Survive*, Routledge, London. pp.369–96.

Nnko, S. (1998) AIDS stigma: a persistent social phenomenon in Mwanza, Tanzania, *International Conference on AIDS*, Abstract no. 417/34159.

Nsutebu Fru, Walley, J., Mataka, E. and Simon, F., Scaling-up HIV/AIDS and TB home-based care: lessons from Zambia, *Health Policy and Planning*, Vol. 16(3), 2001, pp.240–47.

O'Malley, J., Vinh Kim Nguyen and Lee, S., Nongovernmental organizations, in Mann, J. and Tarantola, D. (eds), *AIDS in the World*, Vol. II, 1996, pp.341–61.

van Oudenhoven, N. and Wazir, R. (1997) *Replicating Social Programmes: Approaches, Strategies and Conceptual Issues*, Management for Social Transformation Discussion Paper No. 18. Available at www.unesco.org/most/dsp18.htm (09.04.00).

Parker, R. (2000) Administering the epidemic: HIV/AIDS policy, models of development, and international health, Chapter 2 in Manderson, L. and Whiteford, L.M., *Global Health Policy, Local Realities*, Lynne Rienner, Boulder, CO. pp.39–56.

Pearce, J., NGOs and social change: agents or facilitators? *Development in Practice*, Vol. 3, 1993, pp.222–27.

Rifkin, S. and Walt, G., The debate on selective or comprehensive primary health care, *Social Science and Medicine*, Vol. 26(9), 1988, pp.877–78.

Schneider, H., On the fault-line: the politics of AIDS policy in contemporary South Africa, *African Studies*, Vol. 61(1), 2002, pp.145–67.

Sittitrai, W., Non-governmental organization and community responses to HIV/AIDS in Asia and the Pacific, *AIDS*, Vol. 8 (Supplement 2), 1994, pp.S199–S206.

Smith, J. and Colvin, C. (2000) *Getting to Scale in Youth Adult Reproductive Health Programs*, FOCUS Tool Series 3, Washington, DC.

Thomas, A. (1992) Non-governmental organisations and the limits to empowerment, in Wuyts, M., Mackintosh, M. and Hewitt, T. (eds) *Development Policy and Public Action*, Oxford University Press in association with the Open University, Oxford.

UK NGO AIDS Consortium (1996) *Effective HIV/AIDS Activities: NGO Work in Developing Countries, Report of the Collaborative Study*, UK NGO AIDS Consortium.

UNAIDS (2000a) *Report on the Global HIV/AIDS Epidemic*, June, UNAIDS, Geneva.

UNAIDS (2000b) Local Response Team, Technical Notes 1, 2 (*The Development of Key Notes at All Levels of the Local Response to HIV/AIDS*) and 3 (*How Do Communities Measure the Progress of Local Responses to HIV/AIDS?*), UNAIDS, Geneva. Available at www.unaids.org

UNAIDS (2001) *Reaching Out, Scaling Up: eight case studies of home and community care for and by people with HIV/AIDS*, UNAIDS Best Practice Collection, UNAIDS Case Study, September, 2001, UNAIDS, Geneva.

UNAIDS (2002a) *AIDS Epidemic Update December 2002*, UNAIDS, Geneva.

UNAIDS (2002b) *Report on the Global HIV/AIDS Epidemic*, UNAIDS, Geneva.

UNAIDS with Global Business Council on HIV and AIDS and the Prince of Wales Business Leaders Forum (2000) *The Business Response to HIV/AIDS: Impact and Lessons Learned*, UNAIDS, Geneva.

UNAIDS/WHO (2000) *AIDS Epidemic Update*, December, UNAIDS, Geneva/WHO, Rome.

USAID (1996) *Process Evaluation of the AIDS Technical Support Project of USAID*, July, USAID, Washington, DC.

Uvin, P., Scaling up the grass roots and scaling down the summit: the relations between Third World nongovernmental organisations and the United Nations, *Third World Quarterly*, Vol. 16(3), 1995, pp.495–512.

Uvin, P. and Miller, D., Scaling-up: alternative strategies for local nongovernmental organizations, *Human Organizations*, Vol. 55(3), 1996, pp.344–53.

Watts, C. and Kumaranayake, L., Thinking big, scaling-up HIV-1 interventions in sub-Saharan Africa, *Lancet*, Vol. 354, 1999, p.1492.

Wazir, R. and van Oudenhoven, N., Increasing the coverage of social programmes, *International Social Science Journal*, Vol. 55(1), 1998, pp.145–54.

White, S., NGOs, civil society and the state in Bangladesh: the politics of representing the poor, *Development and Change*, Vol. 30(2), 1999, pp.307–26.

Wilkinson, D. et al. (2000) *An Evaluation of the MoH/NGO Home Care Programme for People with HIV/AIDS in Cambodia*, supported by the International HIV/AIDS Alliance, London.

World Bank (Africa Region) (1999) *Intensifying Action Against HIV/AIDS in Africa: Responding to a Development Crisis*. Available at www.worldbank.org/afr/aids/aidstrat.pdf (19.02.03).

World Bank (2000) *The Costs of Scaling HIV Program Activities to a National Level in Sub-Saharan Africa*, AIDS Campaign Team for Africa, World Bank, Washington, DC.

Recommended reading

Ainsworth, M. and Teokul. W., Breaking the silence: setting realistic priorities for AIDS control in less-developed countries, *Lancet*, Vol. 356, 2000, pp.55–60.

Binswanger, H., Scaling up HIV/AIDS programs to national coverage, *Science*, Vol. 288, 2000, pp.2173–76.

Boyce, W., Johnston, C., Thomas, M., Enns, H., Naidu, D.M. and Tjandrakusma, H., Pathways to scaling-up in community based rehabilitation agencies, *International Journal of Rehabilitation Research*, Vol. 20, 1997, pp.381–92.

Edwards, M. and Hulme, D. (1992) *Making a Difference: NGOs and Development in a Changing World*, Earthscan Publications, London.

Edwards, M. and Hulme, D. (1996) *Beyond the Magic Bullet: NGO Performance and Accountability in the post-Cold War World*, Kumarian Press, Connecticut.

Edwards, M. and Hulme, D. (1997) *NGOs, States and Donors: too close for comfort?* MacMillan Press, London.

Forsythe, S., Arthur, G., Ngatia, G., Mutemi, R., Odhiambo, J. and Gilks, C., Assessing the cost and willingness to pay for voluntary HIV counselling and testing in Kenya, *Health Policy and Planning*, Vol. 17(2), 2002, pp.187–95.

Foster, G., The capacity of the extended family safety net for orphans in Africa, *Psychology, Health and Medicine*, Vol. 5(1), 2000, pp.55–62.

International HIV/AIDS Alliance and GlaxoSmithKline in Global Partnership with HIV/AIDS Communities (2001) *Expanding Community Action on HIV/AIDS: NGO/CBO Strategies for Scaling-up*, London.

Kumaranayake, L., Pepperall, J., Goodman, H., Mills, A. and Walker, D. (2000) *Costing Guidelines for HIV/AIDS Prevention Strategies, UNAIDS Best Practice Collection* – key materials. UNAIDS, Geneva.

Lamptey, P.R., Zeitz P. and Larivee C. (eds) (2001) *Strategies for an Expanded and Comprehensive Response (ECR) to a National HIV/AIDS Epidemic.* (See also www.fhi.org/en/aids/impact/impactpdfs/ecr/ecrfull.pdf).

Myers, R. (1992) Going to scale, in Cooperson, W. (ed.) *The Twelve Who Survive*, Routledge, London. pp. 369–96.

Nsutebu Fru, Walley, J., Mataka, E. and Simon, F., Scaling-up HIV/AIDS and TB home-based care: lessons from Zambia, *Health Policy and Planning*, Vol. 16(3), 2001, pp.240–47.

Thomas, A. (1992) Non-governmental organisations and the limits to empowerment, Chapter 5 in Wuyts, M., Mackintosh, M. and Hewitt, T., (eds), *Development Policy and Public Action*, Oxford University Press in association with the Open University, Oxford.

UNAIDS (2001) *Reaching Out, Scaling Up: eight case studies of home and community care for and by people with HIV/AIDS*, UNAIDS Best Practice Collection, UNAIDS Case Study, September, UNAIDS, Geneva.

UNAIDS (2002b) *Report on the Global HIV/AIDS Epidemic*, UNAIDS, Geneva.

SOME USEFUL WEB SITES WITH INFORMATION ON NGO SCALING UP

Global Fund: www.globalfundatm.org
Horizons: www.popcouncil.org/horizons
International HIV/AIDS Alliance: www.aidsalliance.org
NAM, the European provider of HIV/AIDS information: www.aidsmap.org
UNAIDS: www.unaids.org

Index